I0422975

CALLING ALL HEROES
A MANUAL FOR TAKING POWER

CALLING ALL HEROES
A MANUAL FOR TAKING POWER

by
Paco Ignacio Taibo II

Preface by
Jorge Castañeda

Translated by John Mitchell
and Ruth Mitchell de Aguilar

PLOVER PRESS

Kaneohe, Hawaii

1990

Printed and Bound in the United States of America

Design by Roger Eggers
Cover Illustration by Mirta Toledo
Author photograph by Paloma Saiz

Library of Congress Cataloging-in-Publication Data

Taibo, Paco Ignacio, 1949–
    [Héroes convocados. English]
    Calling all heroes : a manual for taking power / by Paco
Ignacio Taibo II ; preface by Jorge Castañeda ; translated by John
Mitchell and Ruth Mitchell de Aguilar.
        p.   cm.
    Translation of: Héroes convocados.
    ISBN 0-917635-08-6 : $16.95—ISBN 0-917635-09-4 (pbk.) :
    $8.95
    I. Title
PQ6670.A42H4713   1990
863—dc20   90-32134
                                                                    CIP

Distributed by
The Talman Company, Inc.
150 Fifth Avenue
New York, NY 10011

PREFACE TO THE TRANSLATION

For Mexico, the year 1968 was a milestone. It signaled the end of the so-called Mexican miracle, and certainly the end of the Mexican consensus: the imposed or resignedly accepted agreement that there was no desirable or meaningful alternative to the country's authoritarian political system. For Mexico's urban middle-class youth, 1968 was the year that made the difference. Everything happened either before or after "el sesenta y ocho." Finally, for a generation, for those thousands of Mexican students who during three memorable months lived the adventure of their lives, the 1968 student movement was the first awakening to a pleasant and unexpected surprise. Change in Mexico was possible.

Since the early 1940's, Mexico had been the envy of Latin America. It enjoyed political stability: no coups, revolutions or assassinations, presidential continuity— six consecutive presidents had succeeded themselves peacefully and served out their six-year terms—and economic prosperity. The economy grew at an average 6% annually, a higher and more sustained rhythm than in practically any other country in the Third World. Granted, the stability was accompanied by a nearly total absence of democracy. The continuity gave virtually dictatorial, though ephemeral, powers to the incumbent president; and the prosperity entailed widespread corruption, glaring injustice and shameful inequities throughout Mexican society. Still, the "Mexican miracle" was widely hailed, and certainly believed in by those who had wrought it: the politicians and administrators who had run the country for nearly four decades, ever since the Revolution, in one general's ingenious phrase, had gotten off its horse.

The events of 1968, which began as a protest against police brutality and quickly turned into a mass movement for civil liberties and democracy, shook the "miracle" to its very foundations. In stark contrast to traditional protests in Mexico, featuring landless peasants, striking workers, homeless squatters, the protesters on this occasion were the very sons and daughters of the Revolution. The streets were taken over by the middle classes themselves, by the pride of the regime, the proof of its success, the fruit of its efforts. Mexican politicians had always feared the country's social and political polarization: too many too poor, a few too rich.

The idealized, naïve solution was obvious: the creation of a middle-class buffer, better off than the poor, and thus with something to lose, less affluent than the rich, yet more numerous and unlikely to provoke the wrath of Mexico's dispossessed. In 1968, the solution became a problem. The middle class's offspring, those who enjoyed the enormous privilege of free, and at the time still adequate, higher education, were rebelling against the system and against their own fathers who had provided them with this luxury. They were trying to overthrow the system that brought them into this world. For every dignified member of the Mexican establishment, this was the end of their world.

For the youth of Mexico City—the student movement was essentially a phenomenon of the country's capital—and more specifically for those who participated actively, the rallies, strikes and sit-ins which made up the summer's events until the massacre in Tlatelolco Square on October 2nd, were a revelation. Paradox had characterized their political adolescence. In a continent where the

Cuban revolution was in full swing, where Che Guevara had just died in glory in Bolivia, where revolutions, guerrillas and coups d'état were commonplace, Mexico was a country where nothing ever happened. No revolutions—the last one was half a century old, and stale—no coups to struggle against, no guerrilla wars to run off to. If ten years of Charles de Gaulle's Fifth Republic had led Pierre Viansson Ponté, France's premier political commentator, to warn just a month before the May 1968 explosion that "France is bored; its youth are bored," any Mexican pundit could have said the same.

Taibo's book, its heroes and marvelous images of Sherlock Holmes leading a demonstration of Mexican peasants marching on the National Palace, is a tribute to "el sesenta y ocho," to the fantasies it awakened, to the resignation it bred after it was drowned in blood, and to the generation it became an obsession for. The student movement died on October 2nd, at the Plaza de las Tres Culturas, when the Mexican Army fired on the children of the Revolution. Its leaders all dispersed: some faced torture and several years in jail; a few chose exile; many simply faded away. Others still remained faithful to their newly found political vocation. Journalism, union organizing, later the Guerrero, Oaxaca and Michoacán guerrilla groups, grass-roots movements, movies and poetry. The options were numerous, but none as exciting or rewarding as those glorious days in August and September of 1968.

Indeed, the movement gave way to despondency and resignation, more than perseverance or success. Taibo's call to comic- or adventure-book heroes is symptomatic. After the defeat of October 2nd, only fairy tales or adventure stories could heal the wounds and keep the promises of the streets of Mexico City. Years would pass—twenty, to be precise—before the same student leaders, now potbellied and balding, would join the city's teeming millions on downtown streets, all brought together by the 1988 presidential candidacy of Cuauhtémoc Cárdenas. Again, they would lose, although this time around it was a far closer, and less bloody, call than two decades earler.

Taibo's heroes are undoubtedly being summoned again today by the feverish imagination of other defeated, demoralized young Mexicans who see no way to change things in their country, but who still believe that somehow, some day, change will come. Mexico is as magic a nation as ever, and Taibo's heroes are links in a chain. The chain, binding unremitting hope and fatalistic resignation, stretches from the icons of the Spanish Conquest—the brown Virgin of Guadalupe—to the almost religious devotion that thousands of Mexican countryside dwellers feel for Cuauhtémoc Cárdenas today. Now in English, Taibo's *Calling All Heroes* offers American readers a quick and dazzling incursion into these endless meanders of the Mexican soul. It is quite a trip.

JORGE CASTAÑEDA

*To the memory of Emilio Salgari,
suicide, novelist, fellow voyager.*

*For certain special friends who are
far away: René Cabrera, Chema Cimadevilla,
Gerardo Baumrucker.*

*For José Emilio Pacheco, who opened
the doors of the short novel to me and
with whom I competed (from one Friday
to the next), for the better part of a
year in the mutual theft of cigarette
lighters.*

This march of events
obliges the revolution to concentrate
all its forces of destruction
against the power of the state.

VLADIMIR ILICH LENIN

He gathered everyone together and attacked boldly.

AMADIS OF GAUL

Not to admit the taunting rabble in this congress
appears to me a little unrealistic. Don't overlook
the frowning child.

FELIX GRANDE

CALLING ALL HEROES
A MANUAL FOR TAKING POWER

Note

I ASK READERS not familiar with adventure novels to flip to the final pages and read "Appendix One."

For readers unfamiliar with the Mexico of 1969, I suggest going to the last pages and reading "Appendix Two."

Insecure readers (those who think that if they don't read the footnotes they are going to miss something important) are invited to skip to the concluding pages and read Appendices One and Two.

The rest can go right ahead.

Thank you,
PIT II

I
IF YOU WEREN'T HERE,
WHERE ELSE WOULD YOU BE?

For example, on the Bridge of Insurgentes, on the side where that insipid mercury light doesn't disturb the night; over Avenida División del Norte, where the darkness is broken by the constant line of automobile headlights (and there, ten meters below, the Viaduct), like a river of the city with all its roar. You toss the butt and watch it fall, with the secret hope that it will bounce off the roof of a car (and you miss). In a way, with the butt have gone the seven minutes it took to smoke the cigarette, and now you feel like climbing up on the guard wall and pissing on the automobiles. Below, a moving van raises curtains of water as it breaks through the puddles. It's raining again . . .

For example, in the door of the movie theater Roble at the end of the last show. They were featuring, obviously, *The Battle of Algeria*, and the crowd came down the stairs as if anxious not to return to itself, not to leave in stunned silence, but to rush out with the Apache war cries of the Algerians overflowing the Casbah . . .

For example, in the faculty's mimeograph room, hemmed in by the two machines that Eligio Calderón ("The Tricolor") and Adriana had tuned like Swiss watches to produce an average of 2,000 leaflets an hour. In the midst of that fascinating noise and celebrating each new spot of ink on your hands, forehead, nose . . .

3

For example, in San Juan de Letrán, at six in the evening, when the light in the city changes, contemplating a long row of lead soldiers in a showcase and touching with the tips of your fingers the two hundred pesos that you carry in your pocket to buy books in the old Zaplana bookstore: Howard Fast in Twentieth Century Editions at $17.50, and novels by Dos Passos, and *Report from the Foot of the Scaffold* by Fucik, on sale, at seven pesos, and you enter to buy everything, to see it all, to . . .

But you are on a gurney that runs along the corridors, guided by a skillful hand, by an audacious pilot of gurneys, along the racetrack of the white hallways. The fellow ought to notice how a spot of blood is growing on the sheet that covers you. According to the rhetoric of hospital scenes it is obligatory that you encounter a beautiful woman hiding her tears (but not so well that they can't be seen) at the door to the operating room; but there is no door to the operating room, only the spot of blood which grows and the hand that slips from the gurney and falls to the floor, the knuckles bouncing and dragging across the green floor tiles; the orderly wonders whether to stop and/or to push the gurney with violence, his eyes fixed, captivated by the red spot that grows on the white sheet.

You think: they are thorough-going whores, the daughters of Adam climbing over my hands, a hell of a lot of them. And you feel that if you don't moisten your arms with ice water, they are going to rot, they are going to fall off. Could they be termites instead of piranhas?

They're piranhas, the sort that when you stick in your arm you pull out bloody bones . . . But it is a game, a gaming board with the feet acting as markers, moving on the colored squares.

And the loneliness, all the loneliness. The damned spiders and the damned feet of all the buggers in the world.

I am tired. I am not going to be able to read anything this way because I am rather seasick. The trapeze is moving.

A nurse says something while she tears your blue, blood-stained shirt from your body.

"Long live Mexico, children of the Indian whore," you whisper, when they pass you from the gurney to the operating table and a young doctor shows surprise.

A wave of consciousness sweeps over you; you open your eyes and say:

"Of me, they're scared of me . . ."

THE OTHERS' VERSION
A AS IN ACCIDENT

Mexico City, December, 1970

My good Nestor:

You ask me to tell you in three pages about your run-in with the whorekiller a year ago. Accustomed as I am to your wild ideas, here goes:

The version that I have is very exact (gathered from various sources), although it doesn't go further than the most superficial details. Exact, but stimulating.

It seems you left the newspaper office at 5:30.

"To drink a cup of coffee," said the editor-in-chief.

"I've got it," they (the sports writers) said you said after hanging up the phone.

"He left on the run. But that doesn't mean anything. He's always going out on the run," said the office boy.

You had a tape recorder slung over one shoulder.

"From the right shoulder, and it was swinging so much I thought he would hit it on something," said Serafín Nava of the entertainment section, who passed you in the swinging door of the editorial room.

"From the left shoulder. And now who's going to give me back the tape recorder? It's not that it's so important, you understand, but it was an Uher and belongs to the newspaper and here everything is inventoried and so forth," said the administrative clerk.

"Do you have a tape, you eunuch? I said to him, because sometimes a person forgets; and he said, 'I have a pair,' but I didn't understand him," said Serafín Nava.

It seems you left on foot. There's no proof of it one way or the other.

Here a question arises: Who called you?

I had been following your reports. I was buying *El Universal* to do this, to see what in the hell you were trying to do in a world as far from your own as the scandal sheet. And there you went, hasty and precipitate, driven by the same passion as always, hot on the tracks of the whorekiller. He hadn't killed too many, only three, but you had linked the murders together (all of them in disreputable hotels, all of them with a switchblade, all of them in the afternoon), and you had given him the name of "the prostitute assassin" in public and "whorekiller," one word, when discussing it with friends.

Your motives interested me more than what you found out, but in the end you balanced the scales and gave us a story with two characters, you and the whorekiller. Both with the same backdrop: the city we'd learned to know during the Movement of '68.

It seems that you did go on foot. Straight, without hesitating (hesitating at each corner?) toward the fleabag hotel on Artículo 123.

It was 5:50.

"At ten of six, chief, he went inside because, you see, I saw him myself, right? I was standing by the juice stand and turned around and saw him go in, and I said, look, there goes a sucker with a tape recorder worth 3,000 pesos; and later when they brought him out on the stretcher I said, where's that tape recorder? And quick I run up, but it was to return it, to see if they'd give me a little job there at the newspaper. I sure as shit didn't mean to steal it. The law, yes, the cops wanted to get their fingers on it," said Bernabé Quintanar, the juice salesman, whom they found making off with the recorder.

7

"Don't even ask me. They've already asked me the same thing umpteen times," said the hotel manager, who smoked those foul-smelling Veracruz cigars.

You climbed directly to the second floor, using the stairs, and without knocking pushed open the door of Room 203.

"Did you *really* kill them?" says your voice, distorted, but easily identifiable on the recorder.

"Stow that mother . . . Are you the one who writes?" says the voice that later would be identified as the voice of the whorekiller.

"Why, why did you kill them?" says your voice.

"Get that cock out of my face. Sit there on the bed; don't come near me with that sucker," says the voice of the whorekiller.

"It's only a microphone. There's no reason to be afraid of it. You have the knife."

"Yes, but I'm not sticking it in your face."

"Why did you kill them?"

There is a long silence in the recording. A trained ear might be able to pick up the background noise of traffic on the tape. Then, once more, the voice of the whore-killer.

"You wrote all that stuff in the newspaper? About me?"

"Why did you kill them?"

"Don't come near me! Get that fucking mike out of here!"

Then noises are heard, as if the microphone is hanging from the recorder and swinging around the room, striking things. A moan and intermittent breathing that comes and goes.

"Only I would think of shoving a microphone under the nose of a switchblade-packing mama," you whispered, says the stretcher bearer Horacio G. Velasco, of the Red Cross.

The testimony of the hotel manager and a cleaning lady confirms that the whorekiller went down the stairs with the switchblade in his hand (the knife was bloody), holding his head with the other hand. It looked as though he had a wound in the forehead; he staggered.

"Over his eyebrow, about six centimeters, an arc, produced by a blunt instrument . . . the microphone of a tape recorder? Sure, why not, by the microphone of a tape recorder, for example," said Dr. Ruiz, who attended the whorekiller at the Sixth Precinct.

And then:

"He fell. He was coming down and then looked up, and just like that he fell, bouncing on the stairs really hard. It hurt me to watch because he was getting it in the face and the head; but then they told me who he was, the one who killed the women, and I rather liked it. He should have hit harder. Because they may be whores, but there's no reason to kill them," said Severina Balbuena, the chambermaid.

And then:

"We called the Red Cross," said the manager. "I've already told everyone, so quit bugging me."

What happened to you during the half hour that it took for them to find you?

"That, that big pool was left by the young man, the reporter," said Severina; but the tape recorder picked up no sounds until . . .

"That poor dope, he's had it." That voice would be identified as belonging to Ledezma, the other stretcher bearer from the Red Cross.

"No, he hasn't had it," said Horacio G. Velasco, the first stretcher bearer.

Now I'm only left with questions: Who placed the first call? Why did you insist on sticking the microphone into the whorekiller's face?

And that was everything that happened.

Warmly,

PACO IGNACIO

P.S.: As far as this story goes, what happened to the whorekiller, whose name is Andrés B. Domínguez, has no further importance; but I will state, so as to leave no more loose ends than necessary, that he is presently confined in the Castañeda Asylum for the Insane. When you return, you can go and see him.

P.P.S.: The sun . . . tell me, how is the sun in Casablanca?

II
GENERAL WITHOUT AN ARMY

In the city the tanks have been replaced by solitude, but with a similar effect. The wounds seem not to have closed. We belonged to a generation of idiot princes, hemophiliacs down whose skin the blood flowed at the least cut.

Was it you or the whole country which had been split down the middle?

Drying in the sun.

In the hospital the sun entered timidly through the window. You open your eyes and look around: the room, your bed: this Houdini's coffin in which you are confined, and it seems more like some apparatus from a children's park than from a sanatorium (it can be raised on one side or the other, moved around: it has wheels, strange mechanisms to elevate the feet, a call bell and a microphone behind it, bottles of serum attached to the bed, and a vein of yours which carelessly let itself be incorporated into the device), the night stand with apple juice, the few books (they insist you not read too much), the empty white walls.

You think: I am the shadow, the great vampire, the big-assed bird that glides over the Distrito Federal. Above and below the clouds, dozing between gyre and flight . . . Someday the fever will pass. A music box playing a polonaise used to keep me company as a child whenever I had a fever. My great aunt put it beside my bed, and the music of Chopin lulled me and took away my fear, and one day when I wasn't paying attention they took out my tonsils.

THE OTHERS' VERSION
B AS IN BIOGRAPHY

Mexico City, January 6, 1970

My dear boy:

Although I still don't understand a thing, I'm taking advantage of a free moment in my work (goodness, they don't even give us Christmas off) to send you the biography you asked me for. It would have been easier to send you your medical record, which I keep somewhere around here; you already know that writing is not my forte. I suppose that you can make whatever corrections you wish, as many as you wish. But if you wanted something better, you should have written it, since you're the one who knows it best. As you want me to write it, well, let's see what happens.

Biography of my son (as far as I know):

It's clear to me he was born in Morelia, Michoacán, because his parents were taking a literature course (one of your mother's ideas) and since he was two months early, he surprised us while we were out of the Distrito Federal.

Besides being a seven-months baby and giving us the scare of our lives—for he was the first and had a very fixed gaze (imagine scaring your fellow man before you could even see)—everything was normal. It was in November of 1943 and World War II was in progress.

A normal childhood, maybe a little lonely. There were no brothers or sisters. Not overprotected, although too many grandparents to suit me.

Surprising reactions between the ages of five and six. At times a tendency toward introversion that was upsetting to me. No childish fears, no dread of the dark. He stopped wetting the bed very early, much to my pride and comfort (you may remember that according to the pact the nighttime hours were mine). At about two and a half he was no longer wearing diapers at night.

Favorite games: "The yants" (consisted of going out to the patio—we were living in Narvarte, do you remember?—and collecting ants, giving them advice, and letting them go), handball (sometimes for hours on end bouncing the ball against the wall all by yourself until, more from desperation than for therapy I went out and joined you), the bicycle (at six you knew the neighborhood better than the mailman and the milkman put together who, by the way, were great friends of yours), and "school" with two younger neighbor girls.

Primary studies in the private lay school Melchor Ocampo run by my friend Simón Betanzos. Higher than average grades. His mother very proud, I a little frightened. First dance at age eleven (you came home with a face so bored . . . !).

Antisocial adolescence, many conflicts around the home, characterized by irrationality on both sides. Paternal victory on introducing into his room for sparetime reading the first of the science fiction novels which little by little began moving from my bookshelf to his.

I suspect that at age fifteen he was involved in the prep-school demonstration on behalf of the Vallejo railway workers (you had just entered in Preparatory School No. 1, which was located in the city center), and I believe he spent many hours walking around there. More than once I found him walking through the city. In those days it was still possible to meet people in the city without meaning to.

Steady girl friend at age seventeen (1960) when he enrolled in the School of Medicine. A girl from the north (called Cristina?) who used to arrive at the house with his white smock and his books (to you things happened backwards; did you sometimes carry the books of said Cristina?). We discussed medical ethics, we discussed family honor, truth, the meaning of life.

In 1964 he used his vacation to build a room in the patio, into which he moved. With his first job he bought a rug and a phonograph for the room (you were working selling subscriptions to *Reader's Digest*), but I have the impression that he spent more time roaming the city than shut up in the room.

Unsuspected taste for classical music. Accompanied by his mother, he didn't miss a single one of the concerts given by the Bellas Artes Symphony during the season of '64.

The death of Mama. I don't know how it affected him. I was too desperate to take time to find out. I was the shadow of the shadow that I used to be.

He left medicine and enrolled in Spanish Literature.

I regret not being able to say what happened between 1965 and 1968. They were very confused years for me. I know that we ate together, that we shared the solitude of the big house in the San Rafael neighborhood. That sometimes we saw each other during the supper hour and spoke of politics.

I have the impression that he joined the Communist Party in 1966, but I have nothing to prove it.

I have the impression that he fell violently in love, for the first time seriously, in 1967. Again, I can't prove it.

About the Movement of '68 I can say very little. I know that it changed him much more than it did me. That he split his time between school and the room out back, always full of his fevered companions, who spent the night arguing. I know that his fears were not my fears. I can testify that my medical studies enabled me to put three stitches in a head wound he got the day the boys were thrown out of the Zócalo.

I know that I love him, that stranger, you, my son.

I hope that these notes will be worth something to you, besides letting you know that strangers can love each other.

Come back soon.

Affectionately,
PAPÁ

III
INTERVIEW

She was a talkative nurse who moved her hands and winked and squinted while she tossed out words at you. She said things like: How did you sleep? It's time for your shot. Oh, just look at you. Now you've spilt the water. Do you want me to fix your pillow?—without waiting for a reply and mixing questions with orders and advice.

You were seeing her for the first time and you gave her a fixed, troubled look, eyebrows raised and gloomy, but it didn't stop her chatter.

"May I smoke?" you asked.

"Oh, just look at you . . . You don't understand that if you cough the stitches will all come out. Besides . . . "

"When am I going to be able to smoke?" you insisted.

"You have to take these pills," she said.

"Can you get rid of that?" you grumbled, pointing to a white crucifix with a Christ of plastic imitation wood located on the television set in front of the bed.

"The nun will be angry."

"What nun?"

"The one who comes every day."

"No nuns. I deal only with whorekillers."

"Oh!" said the nurse.

Later the doctor arrived. Tall, paternal, smoking a pipe.

"When am I going to be able to smoke?" you asked.

"I knew your dad. We studied together," he replied. He looked out the window and it appeared that he wasn't too concerned about your wound.

You weren't concerned about the wound either. You weren't going to die. Not from this. Not now.

"To smoke, doctor."

"A cigarette after each meal," he said.

You sighed. Now it was just a matter of getting tobacco. The first step in your return to life had been taken.

"You know, if the knife had been two centimeters more to the right, we wouldn't be here talking," said the doctor. He shifted his eyes from the window and they came to rest on the bed, looking at you fixedly.

In these few days. How many? Six, five, four, you had begun to grow a moustache . . .

You ran your index finger over the fuzz on your lip and thought: It was just a matter of centimeters, then.

THE OTHERS' VERSION
C AS IN CONTEXT

Mexico City, March, 1970

Brother Nestor:

You ask me some very difficult things, horny old goat that you are, like what was it like in '69. Like what were we like as if, cold turkey, you had the right to make me go back a year in my life and enter our inferno again. You must think one regains his sense of perspective in so little time; that one can look back without turning into a pillar of salt or a pamphlet . . .

We lived convinced that life wasn't like that, that someone, something, all of us had gotten mixed up in a big mistake. "The Louse" De la Garza organized parties, and we went to all of them knowing full well that you can't squeeze joy out of a lemon. Sad parties in dark basements in the Santa María section, interminable dances in apartments in the Roma and the Napoles districts. Lots of alcohol, recollections of the year before that never went more than halfway, for why remember, why tell someone what he already knows? Never going all the way because, after all, what were you doing with that casual dance or rock partner who stuck to you like you stuck to her? And yet we never missed a Saturday. We had to see each other, to know that at least we were still around: the We Will Conquer Brigade and The Red Group from Prep Schools One and Six, the Brigade Committee from Night School Eight, the Press Committee from Political Sciences, the Chums, the Friends, the Little Bullets.

It's hard to pass from the glory of being everyone to being just an individual, I think now.

You didn't even have a girl friend; you had separated from Gloria, that girl of the large black eyes like mirrors, with an enormous braid and very tight Levis.

As I remember, we didn't resume our studies once the strike ended; nevertheless we dropped into Philosophy, where Tania, "The Squaw," Santiago, and Patricia were; or Economy, where Paco Ceja hung on tenaciously. We didn't discover the wards until the middle of the year, when what would later be called the Comité Obrero Popular (Popular Workers Committee), the COP, began to assemble and which at the end of December was disarmed by the police, who detained a dozen of our companions. And we directed our efforts to the area behind the Airport, to the Aviación Civil, Ampliación, and Caracoles districts, where neighborhood committees had been organized. I remember Alejandro and the work that began in a market. A problem between the administration and the renters, and of our sad intervention, trying to turn the market into a demonstration, a meeting, a student struggle.

Let's change the stage. We wandered alone not only through the Roma neighborhood, but also along the Zaragoza Causeway. At least our city had grown for us. All without much faith. More than anything, we felt a debt toward what we had been throughout the Movement of '68, to those who still were prisoners.

As I remember, we played a lot of chess. We drank too much. You beer, I a thousand and one exotic concoctions (vermouth Cinzano and Don Pancho banana and mint cremes).

We had a job. Do you remember? The adaptation of the novel *A Portrait of Dorian Gray* for television. They paid six hundred pesos a chapter, a fortune.

I waited for Fanny to marry me and so discover afresh my downfall (our downfall), and I suffered from the letters that arrived from Paris. Damned Paris, the ambiguity, the distance, the Eiffel Tower.

We organized a club that was called "The Sons of the Resistance to the Environment." In it were "Crazy" Cendejas, who played tunes from Michoacán on the violin; Paco Ceja Pérez Arce, who kept up his agitations in the Economy Department; and René Cabrera, who wrote inspired poems at that time and then used the paper to fill the holes in his shoes so that the rain wouldn't get his socks too wet.

Rain-bait poems like:

"It was possible to wake up for other reasons."

"No, the rain continues just the same."

It rained a lot, as I remember. That year everything was rain. It rained sometimes, it rained always, it rained too much.

I remember the mercury lights in the puddles; I remember the raindrops licking the windows.

Wait. Seen in another way, I suppose I spent hours watching it rain. Many hours.

Díaz Ordaz, the black monkey, appeared on television frequently. I swore that I would never have a television set.

"Tijuana" went to live in pot paradise. Surprising news arrived of what Pepe González Sierra was doing in the Amazon Basin, consumed by mosquitoes, together with Dulce María. Paco Quinto continued as a militant and had gone to Monterrey. Mario Núñez wrote from Switzerland, where he was involved with partisans on the

Spanish Working Commission and continued a course in survival.

The shadow of the tanks was still in the streets.

You began work at the newspaper. Jonathan "the Werewolf" Molinet and Lucía "Shadows" gave private classes in logic and lived in a rooftop room. Adriana came to my house and made me soup and then spent the afternoon listening to samba records and crying in a corner.

Elisa Ramírez called me by telephone at the most unexpected hours and made dates to walk the streets. She wore very short skirts and long black boots. Moving without direction, we covered the city, hour after hour.

I don't know about you, but I was a sad fellow of twenty who worked at writing magazine soap operas (that sometimes didn't pay), wandered through a city that had been ours and we had lost, rented a room in the Condesa District, had a phonograph and read Faulkner, Rodolfo Walsh, Italo Calvino, Dos Passos, and watched it rain.

PIT

P.S.: I insist, how is the sun in Casablanca?

IV
THE DECISION TO
CALL IN THE HEROES

The first time that the idea crossed your mind, you rejected it without batting an eye, like one who frees himself from an unpleasant thought, like one who drives away an evil dream or consigns a risky job to the trash bin.

Whatever the case, there was something that made the idea stick, perhaps its novelty, something in its very madness that did not allow you to abandon it entirely, even during that first period.

You were napping. You knew that it was late because there was that strange light and the branches of a tree showed clearly through the window. The time could be confirmed because the midday meal was over and the nurse had already carried it away, scarcely picked at, a couple of hours ago.

Then Alejandro Cendejas arrived (nicknamed "Crazy" Cendejas by some of his friends because of his penetrating glance and his insistence on making strange connections between urban life and magical thought), an inspired poet from the State of Michoacán. With him (by accident) was "The Zapotecan Prince," René Cabrera Palomec.

"Hail," said Alejandro, and chose the bed as a vantage point from which to examine the room for microphones, spots on the wall, little boxes of loose medicine that he could make off with.

"How do you feel?" asked René, taking out a notebook and a chewed pencil.

You limited yourself to smiling, which was as good a way as any to thank them for their visit. You didn't feel like talking and napped while they discussed movies and old wives' tales, compared anecdotes about local characters and spoke of the cliques that had little by little been infiltrating the university, controlling first the traffic in drugs, then living off small subsidies from minor officials who had hired gunmen, next allying themselves with the police as informers, and finally consolidating such power they ran through the system getting drunk, violating women, and beating people up.

It was then you said to them:

"I'm going to get everyone together and we're going to fix the mothers."

"There's no one left to get," said René.

"They got us together once and we failed," said Alejandro.

"No, not us," you said.

"Who?" asked René.

"The heroes," you replied.

"Which ones?"

"Mine," you said again.

"You mean there are heroes left?" asked Alejandro, who had always been very skeptical in political matters.

"Why not?" you replied.

"It's time for your medicine," said the nurse.

THE OTHERS' VERSION
D AS IN DOCUMENTS

Esteemed colleague:

After all these lousy months of not hearing from you, look at the kind of requests you make. There's no doubt I have the stuff, so God knows I must send it. The two reports, the one by Revueltas about the political prisoners' hunger strike and the other by Taibo about the mailman from Uruapan. Together they give a good sense of the year of 1969 and the beginnings of '70.

We're in agreement so far. Now, to tell it really well, you should include one of my sports articles. If you want it, okay, I'll send it. If not, I don't give a fart. It's up to you, my friend.

CHUCHO. The star reporter of the sports section of *El Universal*. (Entering the editorial room, third desk on the center aisle.)

NEW YEARS AT LECUMBERRI

José Revueltas

(Fragment from the letter to Arthur Miller, president of PEN CLUB INTERNATIONAL, dated January 11, 1970)

I relate the following in my triple condition as witness, participant, and victim (. . .)

A little after eight on the evening of January the eighth, from our cells in Block "M," where part of the political prisoners from the Preventiva Jail at Lecumberri were being

24

held and in which a majority of said prisoners had been on a hunger strike since December tenth (the rest were distributed between blocks "N" and "C") some comrade from the corridor announced in a tone of alarm that the visitors who had come that afternoon to Cellblock "M" had been detained for more than two hours and not allowed to leave the jail and go out into the street. Our visitors had, in effect, left Cellblock "M" around six and everyone had supposed they were long gone from the prison, so that a great anxiety took hold of us all, particularly those who had waited until the last minute to say goodbye to their relatives. When the alarm was sounded, all of the strikers and a few of their companions who had not joined in the hunger strike, went out into the block's small interior garden to group themselves behind the grate that separates the garden proper from a great double door of iron that in turn communicates with a circular corridor (called a "ring" because of its resemblance to the "alley" in a bull ring) in whose center stands the elevated watchtower known as the "polygon," the gallery on which the majority of the blocks of the prison sharply converge, although others like "M," "N" and "L" make up interior parts of the building, separated from the "ring" by patios, corridors and walls with grated doors, as in the case of the garden of Cellblock "M," which is bounded by two walls at an angle so as to form a trapezium with the line of entrance and exit grates. These details are of fundamental importance in understanding the way in which the events of the first of January occurred. All right, as has been said, more than a score of us clustered at the door of Cellblock "M" to ask the jailors what had happened to our relatives and to beg them to allow our representatives to go out—or at least one of them—to obtain accurate information. The guards flatly denied our request and then, with a vague air of distraction and indifference, left the door and were out of sight down a turn in the "ring" in a matter of seconds. Before our eyes on the other side of the heavy bars there appeared the uncommon sight of a jail that was empty, desolate, without a single guard or person of authority to whom to appeal. A strange and oppressive sensation. To our ears came the distant cries of women and the stifled sobs of children. "Political prisoners! Political prisoners!" they cried in unison. No one could endure such a lament. We beat on the door insanely, some jumped to the other side, others provided with a weight-lifting bar used in gymnastic exercises brought it down on the chains. The locks gave way; now we were in the "ring."

We ran toward the cries. There they were in a corridor, prisoners behind a high door with bars: women, men, children, our visitors. (My wife wasn't there; she had left by chance an hour before the visiting period ended.) But now there was nothing to do, or to attempt, for our purpose was, simply, to talk with the Director or with the Chief of Vigilance: the first, General Andrés Puentes Vargas and the second, Major Bernardo Palacios; with whomever was in authority at the prison, with the aim of obtaining an explanation of events and the liberty of the detained visitors. But already at this moment there was no authority in the prison; or rather, General Puentes Vargas and Major Palacios were there, but they represented *another* authority. They were there, yes, but at the head of numerous and compact files of no less than a hundred common criminals who constituted a powerful "elite" at the penal institution— criminals who were "commissioned" to carry out a wide assortment of duties around the prison: cellblock "majors" and "officials," "guards," "messenger boys," "step-'n-fetch-its," each one of these strange guilds with its respective head at its front, who was, of course, the most proven and feared ruffian of all. The director of the jail and his chief in charge of prison guards, a general and a major who perhaps had proudly commanded soldiers of the National Army in other times, opted this time for the doubtful honor of being those who granted bands of the worst miscreants in cellblocks inhabited by a population of the blackest character, two long hours in which to freely enjoy themselves in the unpunished attack and pillaging without restraint of the political prisoners, which would begin a few dizzying minutes later.

We who had left Cellblock "M" stopped about fifty paces from the point where we would meet, head to head, with the compact mass of "deputies," with the general and the major a short distance from them. We were at the level of Cellblock "E," the "deputies" more or less at the level of "D," and in between, in a "no man's land," the barred corridor in which the visitors were being detained. From behind their gratings the prisoners in "E" covered us with vile insults and shot looks at us of an animal ferocity that was almost unbelievable. One event followed another with sudden, dream-like, fantastic rapidity. Arriving at our backs in a tumult were the comrades of "C," male students who caused surprise—who knows why—because they suddenly looked so extraordinarily young? At the same time the miscreants of "D," for whom the doors of the cellblock had been opened, advanced in an uproar, already armed with pipes, clubs, and bars of iron, through the mass that formed the cordon of "deputies." They began here and there to fall on those of us whom they managed to surprise, unarmed, within reach of their blows. From all sides rained missiles, bottles, rocks, bricks in the midst of a thunder of breaking glass that exploded in fragments, and cries, words, voices and curses of which no one understood anything. Before my very eyes and with gestures that seemed singularly slow and peaceful, a jailor slid his key into the lock of "E," gave a few careful turns with a professional, expert air, took off the chain and then opened the door.

For some seconds those in "E" were caught off balance, perplexed, as if unwilling to credit that strange reality or to dare a step toward the "ring," which under normal circumstances at the jail constituted a step toward solitary confinement in a cell for entire weeks, the feared "mind bender," with which prisoners are punished. But this distrust lasted only for the blink of an eye. Those in "E" came out in an avalanche to join those in "D," and a portion of the latter who had taken the opposite direction from the first, fell on us at a run, on our rearguard, to pin us between two forces. With the instantaneous rapidity of a cinematographic "flash" I made out the figure of the general, who was waving his arms over his head, a black object in his right hand. Immediately afterwards the detonations were heard, hollow, precise, as if produced in a kind of vacuum; the general was emptying his pistol into the air. In different rhythms and in different graduations the uneven random fire quickly became general, seeming to come from all imaginable directions, from above, from behind, from in front, from the sides; the jailors from the "rampart" and from the "polygon" shot in turn. "Take refuge in Cellblock 'M,' in *em*!" we cried. This was the only spot, we thought, where we would be able to save ourselves. Between Cellblock "M," toward which we were running in full stampede, and Cellblock "D," from which the hoodlums had come out to attack us, was Cellblock "N," which was occupied, like our own and "C," entirely by political prisoners. Someone had opened the door that gives access to the patio of "N" and this offered an unexpected intermediate refuge before we could reach the entrance to "M." A large number of our companions immediately took refuge in "N," while the rest of us, now greatly reduced in number, continued to run toward "M," where we entered in disarray, panting, raging, beaten by our own weakness, but also *not* disposed to fight with the common prisoners, having resolved from the very beginning of our imprisonment and by unanimous accord, not to involve ourselves in any battles, which in any case would be, without doubt, a monstrous provocation plotted by the Government against us. Now when we least expected it, we had fallen in the trap of such provocation.

Inside Cellblock "M" there was no way—nor time—for closing the doors, and besides, outside there still remained an indeterminate number of comrades who would not be able to enter "N" and were without refuge or any means of sheltering themselves. A group of fourteen of us, among whom were some from "C," decided to enclose ourselves in Cell Number 21, which was the one offering the greatest security and which the attackers might not be able to enter if we fortified it in a adequate manner. Behind the door of

Cell 21 we piled the beds, a table and as many other objects as possible, and ran home the bolt. Minutes later there began the sacking of the block and then the siege of the cell. We could hear the hoodlums' obsessive and cynical cry of incitation to pillage, entoned with that doleful and repugnant modulation that is their style of speaking, "Get him, get him!" which means the act of getting to the victim as quickly as possible, *getting him*, which is to say falling on him without ado in this opportune moment when he is unarmed and defenseless, and in the most cunning, cowardly and advantageous manner. "Get him, get him!"

Here it is no longer necessary to continue the account. They beat us, stripped us of everything we had on us, pens, watches; plundered our belongings, desks, typewriters, books, beds, mattresses, clothes, manuscripts, everything. Books, books. Of what good to these unhappy people were Hegel's *Phenomenology*, or the *Esthetics* of Lukacs, or Marx's *Manuscripts of 1844*, or the correspondence of Proust with his mother? I was lucky when it came to my first drafts. The floor of my cell was covered with a rug of quartos in disorder, but these, clipped together according to theme and content, were saved for the most part. I lost a cardboard box with more than fifteen folders of notes, not all of them essential, and now I have no typewriter with which to make a clean copy of my work, for I always write in longhand. De Gortari, a doctor of philosophy, on the other hand, unfortunately lost irreplaceable first drafts on which he had invested whole years of labor. He embraced me, moaning with pain, when I met him in his devastated cell.

For me there remains nothing more to say except for the last detail in what has been called the scene of pillage. It's a detail that I can only consider marvelous because of its incredible significance. When at last those miscreants allowed us to leave Cell 21, after having covered our entire bodies with blows and punches, the block was still full of thieves who entered and left with stolen objects. But this wasn't what managed to astound us. The amazing, incomprehensible thing was that the jailors were there among them, walking from one side of the corridor to the other with an indifferent tranquil air, twirling their clubs, which were attached to their wrists with leather straps, as if they were out for an inoffensive stroll. What were they doing there if not to protect the victims of this highway robbery? Very simple: they would direct the traffic of the delinquents, indicating which was the way to leave the unknown block; they would hurry the slowpokes. "Move along, move along, or you'll get lice." I still remember the phrase that the jailor I ran into directed toward me at the exit to Cell 21, meanwhile he bathed me in his smile. "Are you badly hurt, teacher? And he answered for himself: "No more than a few little blows, right?" The title of "teacher," which I never have really liked, on his lips sounded like the vilest filth. No, I am not badly injured, some punches in the face, that's all. I'm not badly hurt.

These are the events that occurred New Year's Day in 1970, seen, as I have already said, by someone who was at the same time witness, participant, and victim.

DEATH BY FIRE

The story of José Refugio Ménez, Uruapan postman.

PACO IGNACIO TAIBO II

BASIC FACTS

Name: José Refugio Ménez Gómez
Employment: Traveling Postal Agent
Seniority: 25 years of service
Age: 51 years old
Marital Status: Married (with several children)
Cause of death: Severe burns cause by autoincineration
Date: April 8, 1969.

A WITNESS SPEAKS

Rafael Alvarez, student at the secondary night school "Lic. Eduardo Ruiz," 16 years old:
"It was something scary to see how that gentleman burnt himself to death. We ran for fear that the can of gasoline which he was emptying over his head would explode, but we didn't realize what was happening until we saw him turn into a torch."
(From the declarations to the prosecutor, April 9, 1969.)

Patrolman David Naranjo Plascencia, Badge 66:
"We were able to do nothing for the suicide, whose death was quick, a question of minutes, perhaps two; it was something truly horrible."
(From the declarations to the prosecutor.)

ABOUT AN HOUR BEFORE

About an hour before I left, he came over and said hello. I saw he was a little nervous. We were in the station. The train for Apatzingán was about to leave. He said to me:

"What's going on? When is it leaving?"—because our train was running behind schedule.

We left about 11:20 and he died at 12:00.

I know that after he died there was a letter by his side to the authorities and to his fellow workers in Celaya, but its contents wasn't made known because the Inspector intervened and kept it.

(*Natividad Rodríguez, postal employee, Irapuato.*)

THE MAIL COACH OVERNIGHTS IN URUAPAN

Cuco took a bus from here (Irapuato) to Celaya and another from Celaya to Acámbaro. There he took the train.

About ten the train arrived at Acámbaro, he got on, and there was a change of postal agents. He traveled alone in the mail coach, where the man he relieved left him his place. I logged in the mail from Acámbaro. It was the train that covered Route 36. Half an hour later it left for Escobedo. He set to work in the cage and about 12:00 the train arrived in Escobedo. About 4:00 it arrived at Celaya. It was early morning. From there he passed the night in Uruapan, where he arrived around 4:00 in the morning, and the next day he killed himself.

(*Natividad Rodríguez.*)

LAST DAY WITH THE FAMILY

At breakfast or dinner we used to talk about things like our studies. One of the last days we were in Guanajuato. It was an unforgettable day, a picnic day at The Dam. From there we went shopping: we bought *charamusca* twisted caramel candy and things like that. The following day was Saturday, so we just fooled around, the boys playing at throwing buckets of water at each other, which they're in the habit of doing, and my dad helping to wet down everybody.

The next day he sent us on a picnic. It was Sunday and he liked for us to get out in the country. Then I gave my dad some money to keep for my fare back to Mexico City (because I was studying in Mexico City to become a beautician).

Then he said to me:

"Be sure to ask me for it later or you'll be in trouble."

When we went on the picnic, I was going to ask him for it, but since he had given my sister a thousand pesos for groceries I didn't. He was going to work . . .

He never returned . . .

(Sobs are heard on the tape recorder. The interview is interrupted for some minutes.)

—Was he nervous those last days?

Just the opposite, he was very happy. The only odd thing was that he spent his time at the typewriter, working to all hours.

He liked writing songs and reminiscences. Afterwards we found out that he was writing letters: to the press, to his friends, to the family.

All his papers were lost.

—Did he talk at home about union problems?

No, at home he didn't talk about that.

—A year has passed. How do you remember him?

There are lots of things: the way he was with his family. The neighbors envied us. He liked for us to have friends and to give parties. He'd help at the parties and say to me: "We're going to have sherbert, we're going to have soft drinks."

(*Interview in Irapuato with the eldest daughter of José Refugio Ménez.*)

33

THE SHIFT BOSS SAYS

"No, the paint isn't there anymore. What he painted isn't there.

"As soon as it was known, they took the mail car and sealed it. Later the authorities repainted it."

(Engineer in charge of the morning express from Uruapan.)

NO TRACE IS LEFT

"They even took down the bandstand. It was there (he points to a spot in the middle of the garden), he stood there, opened the mailbags and sprinkled paint thinner and gasoline on them and then on himself, and he stood on the bags and lit a match."

(The "Old Hat," porter in Uruapan.)

WHAT HE WROTE IN THE MAIL COACH

The night before he died José Refugio wrote four slogans in the car where he was working. Pinky García from the Express Office in Uruapan collected the slogans that were later obliterated by the authorities.

"The employee who asks for a raise in his salary is called a Communist."

"The Revolution was written in blood, the victories of the unions also."

"Let my sacrifice weigh on the consciences of irresponsible public officials."

"Politicians with bank accounts; postal employees with pure promises; our children with hunger and misery."

Besides the four slogans, he splattered red paint in different parts of the coach.

FROM THE NOTES OF A REPORTER

I have been able to establish on the last day that:

He sent his family on a picnic. He didn't wish to accompany them.

He ate alone.

One of his girls returned for her sweater and he was on the point of relenting.

He gave his watch to his eldest son.

He gave the expense money to his eldest daughter and did not allow her to go to Mexico City, where she was studying, asking that she remain for the weekend.

He took the bus to Acámbaro.

Before that he must have put some letters in the mail.

During the night he painted the slogans in the train.

He wrote some notes which, according to the first mailmen who saw the body, contained the slogans.

He bought gasoline and thinner. He spoke with companions.

Although he didn't drink, that night he drank a tequila.

At one o'clock he set fire to himself on the bandstand.

His screams attracted people.

PINKY GARCIA REMEMBERS

That Cuco Ménez was nervous the last day.

That someone had seen him paint the coach the last night.

That it seemed odd that he offered him a swallow of tequila the last night because normally he didn't drink.

That he told him he was going to Mexico City.

He went around telling everyone that he was going to go, and his companions thought that he had been given a better post and was being transferred.

That he had been saying to him for a month:

"Something important is going to happen. You'll see."
(*Interview with Pinky García.*)

COINCIDENCE

"The immolation of said postal employee who had fought for many years for the betterment of salaries and loans for himself and his union companions, coincided with the visit to this city of Lic. José Antonio Padilla, Secretary of Communications and Transportation, on a tour of working conditions through various parts of the State of Michoacán, who was informed of what happened and ordered an investigation."

(From a report in the Herald of Irapuato.)

THE MOTIVES

"Why did your father kill himself?"

"Well, from what they said in the newspapers, so they would give the workers a raise. My father was always talking about that because they belonged to the union. He was helping the workers and said that the authorities never paid any attention . . . We had problems like any other family, but it wasn't for that . . . in the postal service they earn very little . . . my dad had some debts, and it was difficult, but nothing serious . . ."

(Interview with Isabel, the second daughter.)

"HE WAS A GOOD FRIEND"

"Now, only when there is some struggle do they speak of him, of José Refugio Ménez."

"We wanted to raise a monument to him in Uruapan, but the authorities would not permit it."

"He had an idea very deep inside himself, that he didn't tell anyone."

"When they told us about it, we didn't believe it."

"The same authorities prevented the publication of the letters that he left."

"The burning was not in vain."

"His death did some good; there was economic improvement throughout the union."

"At the burial there were secret police because they thought there was going to be a demonstration."

"They sent agents from Mexico City to be at the funeral, which was here in Irapuato."

"After all the legal procedures were over, the wake was held at his house."

"We entered the post office with his coffin, wanting to have a moment of silence, but they wouldn't permit it."

"The mail car he traveled in was 1267."

"He was a very good friend."

(*Juan Martínez and Jesús Aguado, traveling postal employees based in Irapuato.*)

THE TELEGRAM

"At twelve a telegram arrived that said: Señora, your husband has just suffered an accident. I thought the train had been derailed. I didn't think it was any big thing, that he would be at the most injured, in the hospital.

"I inquired of his friends, because he had lots of friends here in the Post Office, and they found out and told me not go . . . but I wanted to go because he had told me that if anything happened, the whole family should go there, and I was insistent . . . I have to go; and they wouldn't let me . . . and they didn't want to tell me that . . . only that it was very serious and that an ambulance from the ISSSTE was going to bring him . . . I was frightened and with all the work left to do on the house, even more . . . and later, I knew . . ."

(*Anita Rosales, widow of Ménez.*)

THE LAST DECLARATION OF PINKY GARCIA

"The sacrifice was useless. Here after the death nothing was said about it. Just the morbid stuff. And the newspapers had orders to keep it quiet. He should have burned himself with the other guy, and then there would have been a real scandal. The bigshot who was on the tour and the next day came through here . . . As it is, it served no purpose here."

HE LIT A MATCH . . .

". . . he was enveloped in flames and cried, he screamed *ay-ees* and shouts that no one understood . . . he screamed."
(From *the report in the Herald of Irapuato.*)

V

LILIANA, GENERAL HEADQUARTERS, LETTERS AND TELEGRAMS

When Liliana arrived, you convinced her.

She was a tall thin girl, almost too much so, and you had met her a couple of months before the encounter with the whorekiller. Appearing in the editorial room of the newspaper, she had first asked for you, then fallen into a swivel chair, where she began telling a story which had to do with words and the police chronical, her graduating thesis in Spanish Literature, her origins in the Argentine (she was the daughter of an Argentinean who exported wines from Cono Sur to Mexico and the United States), and how your reports had interested her. Before beginning the story of the whorekiller, you had written besides fifty or so short articles and contributions to the gossip column, a pair of features: one about a thief who had thrown himself from the second floor of the police station and another about a boy who had killed his little brother and then committed suicide. A pair of bloody disagreeable stories, very much the children of Mexico and very near that idea you had of yellow journalism, that made the pages take fire and burn your hands.

You stared at the girl with the large eyes and the short skirt (Liliana would explain to you later that the skirt looked shorter because her legs were very long), enraged because someone could like what you had written, written in disgust, to piss off, to anger as much as it pissed you off to write it; assumed as a responsibility and an obligation, sin and Christian expiation for being children of this city and not being able to take it by assault.

Liliana endured the attack of your displeasure and decided that she would be able to love you, on condition that you paid for all her love with a pair of kicks to the liver every day.

However, the relationship never got off the ground. You only saw her a couple of times before the final encounter with the whorekiller, and both were a resounding failure. Once you went to the theater and ended up leaving in the middle of the second act. The other you went out for a late supper and couldn't agree on the menu, whereupon you left the supper for a more opportune moment.

Her reappearance at the hospital was received with suspicion, which changed into satisfaction on discovering she was the smiling sister you never had.

Now she was your only card . . . Only in her could you place your confidence for so arduous an enterprise. Besides being faithful, she was turning out to be efficient, and less than six hours later she returned with the following:

Telegraph forms, white paper, two felt-tip pens, one red and one blue, a map of the Distrito Federal (wall size), two boxes of colored tacks (red and green, like the flag), a table-top bell (stolen from a hotel, where it was used to summon the bell boys), air-mail envelopes, stamps, a map of the Crimea cut from the McGraw Hill Atlas, a stamp of the sort that prints the date complete and its purple ink pad, a .38 caliber pistol loaned by René Cabrera, an English-Spanish pocket dictionary, two shorthand notebooks, a box of paper clips, a cardboard filing cabinet, a table calendar, the white section of the telephone directory, a book titled *The Most Famous Codes of the First World War* published by Molino, Barcelona, 1948, the airline companys' blue book, a 1917 Sears catalog, a manual about anarchists and explosives published by Red Dawn in 1922, and a business directory.

All this she distributed about the room and then sat down in front of you with one of the stenographic notebooks and her pencil, very attentive, her hair held back by a ribbon, her short skirt slipping over one brown leg, a half smile on her face.

"You have to swear on your grave that you'll do it, that you'll send every single one."

"I swear," said Liliana.

"And that you'll bring me the registered stubs from the letters and the stamped telegram forms."

"Okay, stop fussing, I said I'd do it and I'll do it. Dictate."

"The first one to the island of Mompracem, Borneo, to a Señor Yáñez de Gomara. 'Urgent you meet me Mexico City, February 28 at the latest. Need a couple of Tiger Companies. Invitation automatically extended to Sandokan, Tremal Naik, and Kammamuri, of course.' "

"Naik, with a *q*?"

"Naik, with a *k*."

"You need a return address."

"The address of the hospital."

"And next?"

"A telegram to Sir Arthur Conan Doyle."

"The one from . . ."

"The same. Send it to Baker Street, Number 221 B. With a note on the envelope that says: Attention Señor Sherlock Holmes."

"Old boy, I'm sure that address no longer exists."

"What was our deal?"

"Okay, okay."

"Text: 'Interested in your presence. Beg you bring Hound of the Baskervilles and omit Watson. Haste is of the greatest importance.' "

"Hey, this is crazy. Do you really want me to send it?"

"Of course."

Liliana stared at you fixedly. You were deep in the pillows, much paler than in the morning, your eyes sunken and feverish. She thought that you'd taken a turn for the worse.

"Are you feeling all right?"

"Perfectly. The next one," you said, "to Jomo Kenyatta, colon, 'Learned you would like to get rid of the rest of the Mau Mau. Request you send them to me in Mexico. Will settle cost of passage later. Eternally grateful, et cetera . . .' "

In the room next door an alarm sounded. The patient had just suffered a heart attack, and in the hallways the chaos that accompanies emergencies was unleashed . . . You continued dictating letters and notes to a Liliana who was each time more nervous, each time less smiling, each time more incredulous, each time more worried.

THE OTHERS' VERSION
E *AS IN EXAMINATION*

Nestor:

I don't have the minutes to that student sectional re-union that was held the middle of October, 1969, to which you refer in your letter. As I remember, those minutes were never kept. I still have (by some quirk you won't believe) the notes for the "examination of the situation" that Julio, Paco, you, and I made a little before leaving the organization. I'm sending you a photocopy of that little paper. After reading them over, I get the impression that we didn't have much to say. Well, it doesn't matter.

An *abrazo*,
Jorge Robles Celerín

NOTES:

1. We persist in acting as if things were not on the ebb. THE MOVEMENT has given way to a small militant sector and the broad militancy that used to exist to a handful of cadres. We persist in behaving as if nothing had happened. Look at what we do in political science at the UNAM and what the "Mamelukes" in physics-mathematics do at the IPN.
2. Basically there has been a failure to find a "way out" for popular militancy, and that is the point. The COP has not prospered, nor the works of the Emiliano Zapata Coalition of Brigades, either. The only logic is found in

the different rhythms of the popular movement (if indeed there is such a thing as a popular movement); we are going at it with the mentality of the Movement of '68.

3. The left continues to fragment into more and more groups. To this is added natural attrition and the continuous desertions of the militants from boredom.
4. The Communist Party has retreated to the most narrow and primitive reformist line.
5. Attitude toward the prisoners dominated by "guilt complexes" and other wholly emotional reactions.
6. Incomprehension by the entire left as to how to consolidate the "social" advance that has been produced.
7. To realize that we are as befuddled as everyone else and that the first step consists in sitting down to think, instead of promoting meetings, assemblies, brigade propaganda as though we were at the peak of the Movement of '68.

VI
SHADOWS AND ANSWERS

The doctor had told Liliana that it was a "complication" and made her leave the room. You had continued to stare at her, with a cloudy light in your eyes, an opaque, but devilishly fixed look, as if wanting to remind her of her promise to put the letters in the mail that very day. She had noticed and nodded affirmatively. In case that wasn't enough, when the doctor pushed her smoothly from the room, she had said:

"Don't worry, the letters will go out today."

The morning was clear, a breeze from the southwest ruffled the red ensign with the tiger head in the center, that crowned the highest crag on the little island in the Indian Ocean.

The room gave the impression of being a combination of opulence and disorder. Here, a silver tray full of precious unpolished stones, there walls adorned with Persian rugs slit by boarding cutlasses. On a table of brilliant sandalwood, various samples of gunpowder on scraps of old Dutch newspapers. In a rickety armchair a European, evidently from the south, dozed with a cup of red wine gleaming in his languid hand. A little further on, in the embrasure of a window buffeted by the breeze, a human shadow whose eyes tried to penetrate the unfathomable ocean.

The second man was a bit younger, a Malaysian of exquisite dress, whose head was covered by a green turbin in which there glowed a ruby worthy of a royal crown. His hands gripped the wood of the window frame, convulsively. A hundred meters below, the sea beat against the base of the cliff.

Sandokan swung his head toward the peacefully resting Yáñez just as Kammamuri entered the room.

The splendor of the Hindu race appeared in the olive, muscular body of the latter, on which were noticeable several deep scars, unmistakable signs of his encounters with the Hindu tiger, one of the most terrible beasts in all creation.

"A message has arrived, Tiger," said the Hindu, for it was by this name that Sandokan, Prince of Mompracem and lord and master of the Malay Archipelago, was also known.

"Something new at last," said Sandokan, taking the letter between his hands and briefly contemplating the strange postage stamp (there is no reason to believe he might have recognized the image of Benito Juárez on the Mexican ten peso stamps).

"Who is it from?" inquired Yáñez de Gomara, stretching and draining the glass of wine he held in his hand.

"We're going to Mexico," replied the Tiger of Malaysia, vehemently. Yáñez, accustomed to the sudden impulses of his friend, who had grown a little rusty during the past season of calm—product of a truce with the English—got to his feet, shook the ashes from his trousers, placed the Colt firmly in its holster, preened his moustache and said:

"When do we leave?"

Under the influence of sedatives that dampened pain and, on the other hand, filled the head with cotton, with a tube that returned the blood lost during hemorrhaging and another that drained the waste accumulated in your body, you scarcely noticed the faces that occasionally came into the room and looked at you. You thought you remembered the warmth in your hand was the product of the presence of your father, who had been in the room for a couple of hours, smiling, speaking with the doctors colleague to colleague, while he held your hand in his without loosening his grip, never letting go.

"Well, Watson, what do you deduce from all that?"

Watson, sitting with his back to Holmes, tried to hide the telegram that he had been reading.

"About what?" asked the doctor, dolefully.

"About the telegram you were reading."

"But you had your back turned . . . You had no opportunity to see . . ." stuttered the unlucky fellow.

"But on the other hand, I had before my eyes a carefully polished silver coffee pot. If this were not enough, I was able to perceive a change in your respiration, an unmistakable sign that you were meddling in papers not your own . . ." said Holmes. "Tell me, what is your opinion of the telegram?"

"I fear it's a trap. The one who writes can't be ignorant of the fact that said hound died in that memorable encounter . . . And besides, you never dispense with my company."

"Watson, Watson," was Holmes's only reply, and he got up disposed to practice for a while on his Stradivarius.

The following day he rented a carriage to take him to Liverpool, where he embarked for New York. Accompanying him was the son of the Hound of the Baskervilles, endowed like his progenitor with an enviable double row of teeth. This time Watson was not next to his admired teacher.

They thought that the sudden kidney infection was going to kill you. You didn't think anything. All your forces were concentrated on your wounded body. You couldn't die now. Not after having found the way out. You let the antibiotics and the fever and the serum and the second operation and the faces of Liliana and your father and your friends pass you by. Meanwhile you waited.

The first time you smiled was three days later, when the nurse handed you an envelope and stood there, awaiting your reaction. You took it, turned it over in your hands, and winked an eye.

"Will you give me the stamp? My nephew collects them."

You assented and there in your hands was the reply of Sir Richard Bachelord Hynes, Acting Commander of the Light Brigade, who had responded to your call from the Crimea.

The next sign that the conspiracy prospered came on Friday, when the doctor, after pointing out that you were out of danger and that all that remained was a brief convalescence, perhaps a little prolonged, but not strict, took from the pocket of his hospital coat a telegram from Dick Turpin, in which he gave the number of the Braniff International flight on which he would arrive in Mexico.

THE OTHERS' VERSION
F AS IN FIESTA

Do you remember, you skinny jerk?

We got together Saturday after Saturday to see if it still felt the same as it had during the Movement. And although it didn't, we returned a week later to say it had all been a mistake, that the parties, even with all the familiar faces there, weren't worth the fifth part of a meeting, of a brigade day, of those assemblies.

"Piss on it," you said, "we have to get used to being alone." But even so, you continued coming Saturday after Saturday. The worst thing is that you didn't get drunk or play the Russian roulette of changing partners or propose political projects in which nobody believed.

You spent your time at the party putting on records so the others could dance, mostly "To the Rhythm of the Rain" by Johnnie Rivers, and smoking unfiltered Delicados one after the other.

You went to the parties whipped. I remember one time you came with a ridiculously high fever caused by the flu, and even so you sat in your corner, smoking and smoking, and putting on records, and sweating it out all red-faced.

I only remember having seen you dance twice. Once at "Lousy" de la Garza's house with an ugly girl from the Polytechnic, who insisted on dancing with everyone. The other time to a slow ballad with Marta, a couple of days before she committed suicide.

That was it.

You were well liked, then and now.

A big hug,
BLANCA

P.S.: I have a job now! I got work as a translator at the Mexican Foreign Business Institute!

VII
A QUESTION, SEVERAL QUESTIONS

Liliana stared fixedly deep into your eyes. Hers were gray-ish and there was a touch of mockery and of humor in their look, a little of complicity and of surprise, a great longing to lose themselves in yours, as if between eyes it were possible to establish a tunnel of truth.

"You really mean it, don't you?" she asked.

"Absolutely," you replied.

You were smoking your afternoon cigarette, the prohibited 1:30 cigarette. The vice was regulated: there existed the legal cigarettes of 8:30, 2:30, and 9:00, the clandestine ones of 12:00 and 6:00, and the smuggled ones (even from your own conscience) of 8:00 and 10:00 at night.

"And how did it turn out?" she asked.

"They were ready and waiting. There couldn't be so much disillusionment, so much defeat. If it could be understood, it could be explained . . ."

Liliana uncrossed her legs and came towards the bed. With her right hand she smoothed the wrinkles in the spread, without taking her eyes from you. You stifled a yawn and looked at the ceiling. Anything to get away from those questioning eyes.

You made up in your head a list of questions that someone ought to answer, one after the other, rapidly, before Liliana could inject herself into your thoughts:

Who washes the dirty pajamas? Technically, how does a radio station function? What is the first name of "Baldy" Osuna? Who founded the Republic of Paraguay? How many spermatozoa in a cubic centimeter? What is the annual petroleum production of Iran? What is the chemical formula for potassium hydroxide? How many kilograms in a hundredweight? In what year was Porfirio Díaz born?

In spite of having your eyes closed, you felt Liliana's lips come near (When did a Russian win Olympic rifle shooting from three positions? In what year was gold discovered in the Klondike? How many pesos does a kilogram of pea-bean coffee cost?) to plant a kiss, the first in several months of knowing you, on your lips. (Did Attila have children? What saints are celebrated the thirteenth of February?) Later her footsteps and her fragrance grew more distant and the door closed. You opened your eyes and stared at the ceiling for a while: whitish, with a small crack that ran from the wall where the window was towards the center.

THE OTHERS' VERSION
G AS IN GUZZLE

My good fellow, just to ask me to write a letter is a sacrifice. To ask that I write you about the last meeting of the COP in June of '69 is a doubly low act. I'm an agraphic. You told me that four years ago. I didn't know what an agraphic was until I discovered it could take me a month to write a flyer. It's only because I love you so much, stud, that I am going to see if I can provide you with that boring discourse.

I arrived with Gerardo de la Torre in a Datsun, and at about four thirty the car konked out on us ten blocks from Marcos Plata's house. I went with a bucket to an apartment building because we needed to put water in it. Gerardo went to Marcos's house after a while because although we pushed, we couldn't move it. Not long after, he arrived on the run with you. You were the color of paper. You told us that you were taking a crap when the police arrived and entered the house. That you went through a bathroom window that gave onto another patio of the complex and from there you lit out. That afterwards on the corner you saw how "Little Fat Girl" and Marcos and the railway workers were brought out under arrest between cops with machine guns.

They were going around the neighborhood because someone had said they had missed some of the people who always went to the meetings. And us there like fools with the fucked-up car. Finally we abandoned it. I had such a scare that the car, which wasn't even mine, stayed there for a month.

After letting the others know, we shut ourselves up with Armando in his house to see if we could find out what had really happened. The COP didn't deserve anything like this because when all was said and done, it had influence only among primary school teachers and railway employees, and it would have been difficult to fulfill the dreams we had at that time of carrying the student movement to the workers.

We had a theory that they had struck out without knowing very well at whom. Later we learned that the conductor Manuel was a stool pigeon and that the day following the arrests he was in a meeting in Pantaco, as if he had never been detained. Then I went to Monterrey and you stayed here, hanging around with the group until you couldn't take it anymore. They tell me that Marcos and the other conductor are just getting out of the can. They've been inside for a year.

And that's what happened, as I saw it.

Monterrey, August of '70
EL QUINTO

VIII

THE ARRIVAL OF THE HEROES
AND THE DOUBTS OF THE HOST

Sherlock disembarked from a great steamer and contemplated, full of admiration, the brown faces that surrounded him; he rejoiced in the melodious accent of the stevedores and the colors of the flowers, fruits, and the women's dresses.

At his back, the dual stacks of the boat emitted a languid smoke. Undoing the top button on his shirt, he loosened his collar and, in an act that was truly atypical, stripped off his tie, allowing himself to be guided by instinct. The hound trotted at his side. Glad to have recovered the liberty it had lost on being shut up in the hold, it evinced its happiness with rapid movements of its tail and thanked the tropics for the return of its liberty and exuberance. Dog of average intelligence, it swore to give its best bites to the people throughout that land.

With his sharp and habitually penetrating gaze, Sherlock contemplated the people, the perfectly calculated indolence of the longshoremen who, with a distant air, unpacked pieces of German machinery. While having coffee under the arcades of the Diligencias Hotel, he decided imperturbably that the palpable reality had nothing to do with what he had read, and almost in the same gesture with which he separated his little finger from the cup to carry the aromatic liquid to his lips, he decided that he had come to learn many things.

Dick Turpin descended from the Braniff airliner, dressed with elegance, but without his garnet-colored frock coat, his embroidered silk shirt, or his mask, which had been placed in his valise. The circumstances had obliged him to dispense with his two flintlock pistols of French manufacture. Instead, he and his men: Peters, Batanero, Moscarda, Tomás Rey and the Knight of Malta, carried a handbag containing 12,000 pounds sterling in gold dust, the product of a raid which had taken place in the County of Leicester, in 1788. With this they could obtain seven pairs of pistols of the best quality, if it became necessary under these new and unusual circumstances.

On arriving at the immigration counter, he took a silk handkerchief out of his sleeve and patted his nose (he couldn't give up everything at a stroke), which made the Mexican official called Gaspar think he had a half gay Englishman before him.

Nothing could have been further from the truth.

The presence of Sherlock Holmes and his hound still floated on the sea breezes of Veracruz when at the other extreme of the country the battleships *Rey del Mar* and *The Tiger of Malaysia* from the fleet of Momprocem, flying Dutch flags, arrived from across another ocean, the Pacific, at the port of San Blas. Here its disconcerted inhabitants could contemplate the disembarcation of 300 Malays, mountain people, and Javanese, who with their wild looks terrorized the beautiful young ladies and hardworking inhabitants of this port of Nayarit.

Yáñez lost no time and, after a nighttime operation that permitted him to unload several culverins and light cannon and 300 carbines and boarding cutlasses, he rented five large trucks and various Jeeps and ordered the departure of his small army for Mexico City. Sandokan meditated uneasily in the front seat of the first Jeep.

"We had to leave nearly 70 men on the boats just because they lacked passports. It's the limit."

The administrative red tape, the rational world of the occidentals, did not sit well with him. Even in moments of calm something like a faint halo surrounded him, a halo formed of desperate charges, of the odor of gun powder and the fierce cries of combat of the Tigers of Malaysia.

"Calm down, brother. Even so, we were able to land more than 300," said Yáñez, phlegmatically.

"But it cost us thousands of rupees."

"Get it into your head once and for all what this country is like. If you remember the letter of our friend, it ought not to surprise you."

While Sandokan seemed to be asking himself what he was doing here, night filled his eyes.

When the noble features of Winnetou appeared in the window of the hospital room, and after him Old Shatterhand, with his fearful Henry repeating carbine and his bear-killing rifle, you couldn't prevent your lips from opening in a smile. Liliana asked you in a whisper:

"And these, who are they?"

"My brother Winnetou and my brother Old Shatterhand," you replied, filling your eyes with the two legendary figures of the prairie.

"Little brother, we have come a long ways at your request," said Old Shatterhand, in Spanish, with a gutteral accent which did not disguise his German origins. The white man let himself drop into an armchair and threw his Stetson hat and a saddlebag to the floor. Winnetou, on the other hand (moccasins, fringed leggings, rawhide jacket), slid toward an accommodating corner, where he sat down on the floor with his legs crossed and on his knees the double-barreled shotgun adorned with silver nails. From the window could be heard the pawing of the horses.

At that moment, and for the only time in the course of this history, you doubted. Were you going to do it? Were you going to unleash the fury of the heroes against the powers that be? You, a member of the beaten generation, would you be capable of putting together a victory?

The nurse entered the room and after looking with a combination of suspicion and disgust at your two guests, she gave you your medicine, waited for you to swallow it, and went out, saving her insipid chatter for a better moment.

"Did you come alone?"

"You didn't say anything about it in your letter. All we have with us are a dozen *mezcalero* Apaches. They're in the park, taking care of the horses and resting.

Then, to make sure this was true, you got out of bed and limped toward the window. Liliana gave you her hand and Old Shatterhand supported you by the elbow. And yes, around a fountain where 14 mustangs were watering, a dozen *mezcalero* Apaches basked in the sun. Little by little the old men from the nearby annex, the asylum, had left their rooms to share a bit of the sun with the Indians. One of them was trying to convince the latter that the horses of Andalucía were better than theirs.

And here all doubt was banished.

"With your help we're going to stir up a real hornets' nest in this town," you said, to your new companions.

THE OTHERS' VERSION
H AS IN HOOFPRINTS

Nestor, I am going to accept the supposition that it's just as you say: strange things happened in Mexico City between the 14th and the 26th of January, 1970. At that time I was in the hills of Puebla, doing radio programs about witchcraft and shamanism and didn't hear about it. Since receiving your letter, I've been nosing around and here are the surprising facts I was able to collect.

1. There was a widespread rumor that a military coup was about to take place. It was said that the general in charge of the Jalisco zone had gotten the trucks and tanks out on the highway, that he was left behind and ended by committing suicide. Also there was talk of a supposed insubordination by Hernández Toledo, the general of Tlatelolco; and lastly, it was rumored that there had been an uprising in Tlaxcala. Rumors and nothing more, impossible to confirm.

2. It's true that on the 21st the Cathedral bells sounded a call to arms. There are no explanations.

3. I spoke with a buddy at the Science Institute (Rolo Díez) and he told me that on the 18th there was a cloud of ash over the Distrito Federal. He believes it originated in the Azcapotzalco Refinery. I spoke with the public relations chief of the Azcapotzalco Refinery, and he threw me out for a lunatic.

4. The President made no public appearance between the 22nd and the 26th. Not even a register of his audiences at Los Pinos could be found. Later it was said that

he had suffered a detached retina. Afterwards, that the injury had originated in a lesion produced when a 20 centavo piece mixed with confetti had been thrown at him during a parade. Of course, it was also said that a double took his place. If that was true, the double turned out to be as sinister as the original.

5. Channel 2 stopped transmitting from 11:45 to 1:30 at night between the 24th and 25th. No explanation was given for the technical failure.

6. I was told there was a shootout in front of the Chamber of Deputies and a "cavalry charge" (sic!) on Calle Luis Moya. I obtained the first information in a canteen on Bucareli, called La Favorita, and the second I was given by a guy who was absolutely soused, who at that time couldn't distinguish between his sister and a horse.

7. Many people have spoken to me of a riot in the San Cosme market place, although no one could name the cause. Of course, the papers said nothing.

8. Your dentist, that crazy Maripi, informed me that she had been going out with Dick Turpin, a very agreeable Englishman, and that she even served as his chauffeur in a bank robbery. You know Maripi. If she tells me she practices witchcraft in the dentist's chair with López Rega, I believe it.

9. I'm beginning to suspect that something strange happened during those days. The final proof was when I spoke to your friend Liliana, to crazy Javier (Bighead's brother) and to Pedro Páramo; and the three of them acted crazy and went off without answering, turning more mysterious than Chinese policemen (before Mao Tse Tung).

10. Take away my doubts. You were in the Distrito Federal, right? You didn't go to Casablanca until the 26th, did you? What was it that happened? If I had

known that this city of shit was going to turn interesting,
I wouldn't have gone to Puebla.

Tell me all about it.

Rene

IX
STRATEGY, INFIRMARY, AND MAU MAUS

Contrary to what future detractors may suggest, you thought that the insurrection was a very serious thing, and you began your convalescence disposed to create an operational master plan, a strategic project that would allow you to sink your teeth into the evil Mexico. It was not enough to enlist the obvious centers of power (together with those not so evident), it was necessary to trust in the spontaneity of the race (because if you didn't believe in that then what the hell could a veteran of '68 believe in), and to add to it a watchwork mechanism, two or three touches of humor, a good dose of the absurd, and much vengeance. All the operations had to be linked and given a meaning. Put together. For this, you and your little pencil took advantage of the hospital afternoon to set up the greatest commotion this valley would ever know. Comparable only to the arrival of the bearded Centaurs of Andalucía, Castilla and Extremadura, that accompanied Don Hernando Cortés, the approach to the presidential chair of Villa and Zapata, the earthquake of '57.

To your misfortune, at the hour of creating the master plan, you discovered that the summoned forces were very few; besides, you didn't know for certain who would respond to your call. Because counting must be done on the fingers and not in dreams.

The sun beats against their backs. The blows of the horses' hooves on the asphalt highway, the soft whistle of Doc Holliday and the rhythm of the six men riding.

The highway signs are written in Spanish; the sweat is familiar, that soft itching of the hands that indicates the beginning of an adventure, the nearness of danger.

The oiled pistols stuck in their cartridge belts, the rifle hanging from the saddle, the small sawed-off shotgun which the doctor caresses with his black gloved fingers, adding life to its bluish luster. Morgan scratches his horse's back and Virgil dreams of a redhead that slept in his bed the last day in Abiline. Bren chews a piece of straw and lets his eyes become one with the parched barren landscape. Wyatt Earp accompanies Doc Holliday's song with a soft movement of his head.

A Hercules moving van passes them. The driver sticks his head out of the window to engrave on his retinas the image of the six Gringo cowboys trotting along at kilometer thirty-three of the Querétaro Turnpike. A little further on is a wheatfield, and there they meet a landless farmer who is working it as a hired hand.

The elements have united to give you a tranquil afternoon. Neither friends nor hospital personnel have appeared in the room. This was fine so long as you hadn't needed someone to bring the map of Mexico City nearer the bed, but now you rang the bell with desperation, in order to convert a nurse into an aide-de-camp. On the third ring, a face black as night appeared through the half-open door.

"Mr. Nestor, I suppose?"

You nodded and the man entered the room. Behind him a second and then another. At first glance they appeared to be young executives from developing African nations, visiting a hospital, but you shrewdly discovered that underneath their European vests and their well-cut pants were short machetes, kitchen knives, sharpened razors capable of cutting paper. The Mau Mau were with you.

The war chief introduced himself as N'Gustro and indicated how the hierarchy of authority altered in different situations: in conversations on protocol it was necessary to speak in the plural, directing yourself to the war chief, to a man wearing a leopard skin cap (whom you discovered was the witch doctor when he began poking around in the room, in the medicines, and even in your wound), and a third character who was not present. For military problems it was necessary to deal with the chief; and for problems about splitting the booty, with the bookkeeper, a little African of light complexion called Styron, who took a calculator rapidly from his pocket, with an obvious desire to introduce himself.

Little by little the room began filling with Africans. Several sat at the foot of your bed, observing you and making comments in a musical dialect. And the invasion had extended much further than the room: the maternity ward in the nearby annex, the great crystal front of the incubator, the cafeteria on the lower floor, the little park in front, and even the game room of the asylum had been invaded by the 450 men of the Mau Mau sect.

After having resolved the problems of protocol and evaded the delicate subject of splitting the booty, you had succeeded in directing the conversation to the problem of whether or not they would use war paint on their faces, when a young nurse made her way fearfully among the Mau Mau to bring you two small red pills and a glass of water.

Dividing her attention between the little plate of medicines and the suddenly smiling faces of the Mau Mau, she managed to say:

"Are they friends of yours, Nestor?"

"Students, students of mine. From when I gave classes in Spanish at a school in Kenya," you replied proudly.

Hours later the poster hangers of the Mexican Arena did their duty by fixing showy strips of paper on the walls of the city, on which was announced the presentation in Mexico for the one and only time, and within a week, of the most spectacular troupe of lancers in the world: the Light Brigade. Directly from the Crimea, to the three rings of the Mexican Arena, for one time only and within a week.

You slept well, tranquilly, full of that sensation of placidity which comes from knowing you're not alone in your madness.

THE OTHERS' VERSION
I AS IN INERTIA

Ah, what a dear Nestor:

I am writing you in a free moment between breast feeding, changing diapers, and preparing bottles for the twins. Imagine me like this, please, just imagine. Nothing like the girl who existed two years ago. The woman I am, please, Nestor.

I don't know why you remember me now and write me a damned letter with two frigging lines: *Tell me what we had going; what was it like?*

What we had going was falling one onto the other, just the same as if we had fallen on the ground. There was such a great emptiness around us and around all our people that any kind of relationship that went to bed and walked around that horrible, nauseating Distrito Federal (and how beautiful it had been in '68 and how shitty were the streets and the people and the city in '69), seemed like love.

And the truth is we might better have fallen to the ground.

From wherever you might be, send a kiss to my sons, to me (the woman you no longer know), even one to my husband, Pablo (do you remember Pablo?).

What we had going was like falling on the ground, and the worst thing is that our butts didn't smart; something else did.

GLORIA

X
VERY IMPORTANT MEETING IN THE HOSPITAL ROOM

"May I smoke?" asked Holmes.

You assented. He was an unusually thin man, almost two meters tall. He looked a little like Basil Rathbone, and of course without that ridiculous little hat with which the movies had stereotyped him. Aquiline nose which gave his face a perspicacious look, firm lower jaw, dreamy air that fooled the observer who was not able to perceive the tension hidden in the muscles. Hands spotted with ink and chemical burns. Now, the spark of genius in his glance.

"I understand that your wound is much better," he said, lighting his pipe.

The room filled with a thick acrid smoke.

"They've told me there is no danger," you answered.

For an instant you and Sherlock contemplated each other in silence.

"What is my part in this story?" he asked, suddenly.

"Your scenic presence, your elegance, the assassination of Díaz Ordaz."

"Strange propositions . . ."

"I suppose all this is going to be a little out of the ordinary," you replied.

Sherlock nodded. Once more you both were silent.

The arrival of Wyatt Earp and Doc Holliday was preceded by the jingling of their spurs in the hospital corridors.

They were cold-blooded men with imposing moustaches, their revolvers hidden by vests that in turn were covered by black coats of full, old-fashioned cut; favoring discretion, they had not worn cartridge belts. Myth had given them steely looks, and myth had been right.

"Here we are," said Wyatt Earp. "We were summoned and here we are."

You stretched out your hand from the bed and they both shook it, transmitting a feeling of solidarity through the warmth of their grips.

Later Dick Turpin arrived, and Sir Richard Bachelord Hynes in his blue cuirassier's uniform. Doctors and nurses patrolled outside the room, but they didn't dare to enter.

After introductions, the group remained silent, smoking, looking out the window once in a while or going to the bathroom to empty the ashtray that Liliana had stolen from a hotel. It was your moment of glory and the tension did not permit you to enjoy it. Winnetou and Old Shatterhand arrived preceded by the sound of voices. Their carbines had scandalized the hospital personnel, and you felt obliged to drop the phrase: "They're part of a movie, you know." Enigmatic, but sufficient for the doctor to let them in.

Lastly, Sandokan, Yáñez, and Kammamuri made their entrance, and instants later N'Gustro arrived in a state of anguish.

"I can't find them. They've disappeared."

From his disconnected talk you were able to determine that to kill time the 450 Mau Mau had taken a tourist jaunt to Teotihuacán and gotten lost.

"Let's take it calmly. They won't be necessary until tomorrow afternoon," you said, to calm the war chief.

You ran your eye around the room, trying to create the necessary pause that precedes great occasions: in the armchair Holmes placidly smoking his pipe, his style cold-blooded. In the window Old Shatterhand and Winnetou, the moral gentlemen of the Southwest, they who had succeeded in going through the white-Indian wars without being stained with racism. Near the bathroom door and leaning against the wall, Wyatt Earp and Doc Holliday, the fastest guns in the West and cool customers. Seated at the foot of the bed, smoking and smiling, not from sluggishness, a personality no less passionate than the rest, Yáñez de Gomara, the best chief of anticolonial resistance in Malaysian seas. Next to him, Sandokan, the Tiger. Sitting on the floor Kammamuri and Tremal Naik, placidly waiting; and against the wall to one side of the door, seated on three stools provided by the hospital staff, Dick Turpin, the commander of the Light Brigade, and the war chief of the lost Mau Mau. It wasn't a bad team.

"Well, gentlemen, this has to do with seizing power," you said.

THE OTHERS' VERSION
J AS IN JUSTIFICATION

The nitty gritty, I don't have it. I gave it to you, you lost it, I lost it, I gave it to that skinny little girl I was so in love with. But in view of the fact that our chums here say you are reconstructing something important (they say it because of the variety of mail you send and receive), I'll redo it for you.

THE MOTIVES OF THE REVOLUTION THAT NESTOR IS FORGING
For us the old truths no longer hold any comfort:
  we burnt the pages of the manual in the torches
  we made loneliness with kitchen recipes
  we created feelings out of multitudes
  we learned to think: Fatherland
  without the word's
  filling itself
  with cherubim
  marching to the beat of the national hymn.
We discovered a country
  and we acquired our debts.

Wasn't it something like that?"

An *abrazo,*
RENÉ

Mexico D.F., Colonia del Valle, April of '70

XI
OF THE INSURRECTION

When dawn broke the following day, the inhabitants of Mexico City saw "a spike of fire, like a flaming swamp, like an aurora; it showed itself as if it were dripping from, as if it were throbbing in, the sky."

Hours later a rain of ash fell on the neighborhood of Azcapotzalco.

Both events went unnoticed by the majority, and those that saw them were convinced of their accidental nature by the noon television commentators.

But other signs were in the wind. Perhaps not as visible as the two preceding, but equally full of portent.

A little before two thirty a pair of men in masks, decked out in red coats embroidered in gold and white, broke into the room where the bellringer of the cathedral slept and after threatening him with eighteenth century pistols, robbed from who knows what museum or stall in Lagunilla, forced him to ring the alarm bell. Then, just as they had arrived, they disappeared.

Half an hour later, to top off that morning of strange situations, three hundred lancers on horseback left the esplanade in front of the Museum of Anthropology and passed at an easy trot down the Paseo de la Reforma. On arriving in front of the U.S. Embassy, one of them opened a sack that he had hanging from the saddle bow and took out a dead pig and threw it in front of the grating at the entrance.

The scene was captured by the camera of a Colombian tourist, who sold the photo to *Time-Life* for 600 dollars.

Toward four in the afternoon it began to rain. Hours later the insurrection began.

THE OTHERS' VERSION
K *AS IN* KULTUR

I add the little notebook of quotes that the brothers and sisters put together and that only I took the trouble to copy during the past year. Frankly I forget what we meant to do with it. I pass it along because you reminded me of it. It's a combination manual for survival in the jungle of the Distrito Federal and a course in local philosophy.

An *abrazo,*
RENÉ

There too we died again.

ALEJANDRO CENDEJAS

Armando Manzanero began his fight for good taste from a very early age.

A record sheath from a Capital record

Only the chastity I was able to maintain throughout this whole period enabled me to persist in my task without a break in health.

JOSÉ VASCONCELOS,
Minister of Public
Education, 1921–1924

Comrade life, let's walk faster.

V. MAYACOVSKI

But let's return to that atmospheric violence, to that violence as natural as breathing.

FRANZ FANNON

Deeds are what decide, not illusions. We want to show a face, not a mask.

LEON TROTSKY

The conscience is wiser than science.

BATMAN/*in the Editorial Novaro version*

Tokyo (AP). Juan Máximo Martínez, Mexico's best distance runner, was in a bad mood owing to his defeats in a series of Japanese races—according to a report in *Hochi Shimbun*, a sporting daily of large circulation in Japan.

The races were of little consequence and it is inexplicable why Martínez, one of the best runners in the Mexican Olympics of '68, should be so dejected.

The reason—according to *Hochi Shimbun*—is that Martínez had promised President Gustavo Díaz Ordaz that he would win the events.

Martínez took second place in the 5 kilometers in Hiroshima and also second place in the 10 kilometer event that was run during the Carnival of Kobe, on April 29.

According to the daily, the Mexican President had promised Martínez, on his return to Mexico City, to install running water and electricity in the house where he lived.

The Japanese added that at the end of the race Martínez looked only at the ground and didn't even wipe off the sweat. The saddened runner could only smile when he spoke of the tartan Mexican tracks.

He said with pride that in Mexico there were six, and he wondered how it was possible that in Japan, where everyone had running water and color television, there were none.

> I am not dead there then. I am alive here now.
> LUIS MARTÍN SANTOS

> One can also be a scoundrel from loneliness, from sleepiness, from fatigue.
> JORGE ENRIQUE ADOUM

> Be silent and smile, nothing is the same.
> ANGEL GONZÁLEZ

Three items about the wind:

1. The wind blows where it will;
   you hear its voice, but you don't know where it comes
   from or where it goes

   SAN JUAN

2. You are only wind, when you complain
   You are wind if you roar or murmur,
   Wind if you approach, wind if you go away

   VICENTE RIVA PALACIO

3. I am tired of chasing the wind

   PIERRE SCHOENDORFER

Pornoproverbs:

He who carries a good stick
is bound to leave you a memory

Don't blow
a gift horse's trumpet

Guadalajara on a plain
and you peel my turnip

Shrimp that sleeps
go and fuck your mother

Neither love nor surfeit
loneliness nor the wind
can hide us now:
not even from ourselves
                                    P.I.

. . . all these signs and others by which the natives' end and
finish were foretold, because they said the end must come
(. . .) and new people had to be created.

MUÑOS CAMARGO, *History of Tlaxcala*

XII
OF THE INSURRECTION (II)

When the three school buses and the Social Security Jeep stopped in front of the barracks, the sentry stretched himself and gave them a bored look: it was only three school buses and a Jeep full of Malaysians and wild men from Borneo armed to the teeth.

A rutabaga vendor, who when all was said and done would be the only credible witness, observed how a group of men ("like Indians. From India? No, like from Oaxaca, but with the look of bad-asses") lowered a bronze cannon from one of the trucks.

"You can't park here. This is a military zone," said the sentry to Sandokan and Yáñez, who were getting out of the Jeep.

The Tiger of Malaysia was dressed in pantaloons of red velvet and a black silk shirt; his long hair was held by a red band at the forehead. Yáñez, with two Colts in his belt, looked smilingly at the sentry.

Sandokan drew a Malay kris and placed its point, poisoned with the juice of the upas tree, at the throat of the sentry who, without questioning it, let his M1 fall to the ground.

"Forward, my Tigers!" cried Sandokan, and was answered by a howl of fury and delight.

Then a firestorm was unleashed. The earth boiled. Pistol in hand, the Tiger directed the first combat groups, throwing sticks of dynamite that destroyed casemates and buildings. A group of Tigers guided by Kammamuri

77

climbed the water towers and from there acted as sharp-shooters, killing all the soldiers who tried to mount a resistance. Blood spewed from a thousand wounds, meanwhile the horde raked the installations of Military Field Number One with fire and lead.

The embers were still not out in the military zone when Dick Turpin, at the head of his six faithful companions: Peters, Batanero, Tomás Rey, Moscarda, Pat, and the Knight of Malta erupted in the Chamber of Representatives with their pistols drawn, and in place of the traditional "Your money or your life" ordered the upright public servants to take off their pants. In the midst of the confusion this provoked, with pants dragging on the ground, the Forty-Seventh Legislature paraded down Calle de Donceles, guarded by seven masked gunmen conducting them to an unknown fate.

The official government had still not recovered from its disorder when the forces of the Army of Reconquest, as they had been baptized, delivered their next blow. Old Shatterhand and Winnetou, armed with their mighty carbines, began to shoot, just before eleven, at the Offices of the Judicial Police of the Distrito Federal, causing disorder among policemen and onlookers.

If this were not enough, a half hour later, 600 riders with lances at rest left the Mexican Arena in perfect formation and after a wild cavalcade through the Colonia de los Doctores and the center of the city charged the barracks of the grenadiers, which was located on Victoria.

A commander of this illustrious body, after the first surprise, tried to organize the defense and placed two lines of grenadiers in the street, who with Mausers and gas canister launchers tried to impede the second charge. The brigade began its advance at a slow trot, then began to accelerate, its lances pointed at the blue chests of the forces of order. The noise of the horses' hooves mixed with the sounds of shots and the dry bursts of gas bombs that flew toward the lancers. In the midst of a cloud of gas and smoke, the charge broke the ranks of the grenadiers. The lances skewered bodies, strung the police like beads, and threw the sad remains against the electronics stores on Calle de Victoria. Tearful, but content, the inhabitants of this area began throwing flower pots and pieces of furniture from their windows at the fleeing police. A third charge was unnecessary.

The last act of the day caused a groundswell of rumors to run through the city. It was said that the President of the Republic had died during a reception at Los Pinos, that he had been attacked by a ferocious mastiff whose eyes shot fire. The mastiff, which had been brought to the reception by a British gentleman, leapt at the throat of the first magistrate, ripping it out with a single bite. It was said that the President's last words were: "Oh, nanny."

Two things worried you: one that the Mau Mau were still lost in Teotihuacán and the other that the moment would soon arrive when you would know if the loyal and noble people of Mexico City would join the insurrection or would remain as observers of such fantastic events.

Of all this and much more you had been kept informed throughout the first day of combat. Liaison came and went between the sanitarium and the battlefronts, and you kept track of and sent orders to the forces scattered throughout the city.

To kill time, you ordered the execution by firing squad of the owner of the television channels, and in remembrance of the shootings on the Cerro de Las Campanas you placed the manager of news on his right and on his left the director of children's programs.

As a just seal to a day full of sensations, emotions, and triumphs, the representatives were thrown into the Grand Canal during the night.

THE OTHERS' VERSION
L *AS IN LEGEND*

Letter to the great Nestor, from little Laura (dated the middle of 1970 in the Distrito Federal, written in the Roma neighborhood on a sunny day):

They tell me you write letters and notes asking friends to tell you their stories, to send you news clippings and to tell you about yourself. You haven't asked me for anything; that's why I dare to write. If you had asked something from me, I would have been paralyzed and would never have been able to set one letter after the other.

I'm going to tell you how the great Nestor looked from the viewpoint of little Laura. You remember little Laura? You remember how you patted me on the back and gave me chocolates and novels by Simone de Beauvoir when I went to your house and told you that nobody loved me? You remember how you complained bitterly that I had adopted you as a father figure and spattered your shirts with foolish tears every week?

Maybe that is why I am the only one who can tell you the legend of the great Nestor.

The Great Nestor never cried. When it appeared that he was going to cry, he raised his eyes and looked at you, frowning and very serious for a while; then he smiled. He never cried in public and according to what I found out from Gloria, in private either (not in her privacy), and as René and Paco Ignacio have confirmed, he never cried when he was drunk (so much they have said).

The Great Nestor was useful, had studied three years of medicine and knew how to cure colds and tonsillitis; he could distinguish between menstrual cramps and stomach ache and knew how to inject antibiotics (at sixteen years this was as close as I could get to you). It was for these reasons that we liked him more, because in addition to reading poetry and organizing lightning demonstrations he was useful.

The Great Nestor was strong. He was always ready to listen to us and to love us at a distance. I suppose that had something to do with the fact he owned more time than we did; his days lasted longer (did you really sleep less than other mortals?). He always had time to walk around with us or to read what René had written, or to edit a pamphlet, or to work and garner a little money. The Great Nestor was strong and lasted a long time (like Mimi lollipops).

It was said that the Great Nestor made decisions and converted them into deeds. This was important for us mortals who filled notebooks with projects that never got done and elaborated lists of plans, knowing they would drown on paper. One day the Great Nestor decided to be a yellow journalist, left the house and returned three days later with the job and his first article. The Great Nestor decided to stop smoking for a month and threw his butt out the window, and I swear he picked it up 31 days later. He decided to leave the organization, went to the cell meeting and said: "I'm going. This doesn't work. I can't explain it to you." And he embraced everyone and left.

The Great Nestor was tough, didn't wear an undershirt, ate junk food, read not only what he liked, but also "what should be read," never asked favors, was punctual, could go all day without speaking, shaved himself every day (without soap, dry).

The Great Nestor was a legend: in 1968 he had stood up to the grenadiers in La Ciudadela, with blows, rocks, and clubs.

But, above all, the Great Nestor had a magnetic smile ... After passing an afternoon in silence, holed up in a corner of the room, he was able to get up, look at us and smile, as if sharing a great discovery.

These are the things that I tell some of his friends. The legend of the Great Nestor. The fact I can tell it to you, too, shows that now I am 18.

Don't be sad, don't feel lonely.

LAURA

XIII

JUDICIAL POLICE
AND MUSKETEERS

First the fat one entered. He looked at you fixedly for a while and a cat-like smile appeared underneath his Pancho Villa moustache.

"Morning," he said.

After him, the pockmarked one. He wore a very ample navy blue shirt with a zipper. He looked at the bed with a bored air, lifting his eyes slowly toward you. They stopped when they met your eyes and then continued upward as if he had lost what little interest he might have had. The moustachioed fat one sat down at the foot of the bed, obliging you to pull in your feet.

"Let me guess," you said, "lottery ticket salesmen? A romantic duet? The assistants of Nacho Trelles?"

"Hit him one," said the pockmarked one, without looking at you.

The fat one gave his feline smile, ambled toward the head of the bed, and without any warning took a squad pistol out of his belt and destroyed the bottle of serum with the butt. The pieces of glass dotted your pillow.

"You don't hit wounded people. You're a real ass, Malpica," said the fat one to pockmarks.

Once again that feeling along the spine, the cruel tickling, constricted, that rose through the vertebrae.

The pockmarked one inspected the levers and cranks at the foot of the bed and began to turn them. The lower end of the bed pushed up with heavy creakings. You placed a hand over your gash as if wishing to protect it. The fellow moved the other handle and the head lifted. You felt as if your body was going to turn into the interior of a sandwich, trapped by the bed's mechanisms.

Meanwhile the fat one opened the drawers of the night table and without giving them the least importance, dumped the maps, pencils, books, medicines, and notebooks on the floor.

You jerked out the serum needle just in case they intended foul play, and threw it in the pockmarked man's face.

"What bad manners," he commented.

The door opened at that point to allow the entrance of the night nurse, who contemplated what was happening with terror.

"What are those gentlemen doing?" she cried.

"Judicial police," answered the fat one, showing a wallet with a shiny metal plaque.

The pockmarked one wasted no time in explanations and, taking her by the arm, threw her in the armchair.

"What's your name, baby?" asked the fat one, of the terrified nurse, whose fright was giving way to anger and now looked at them with a frown.

"Silvia Singer. I am the night nurse in charge."

"Uh, what good nights the sickies must have here."

"Consider yourselves dead," you said suddenly, trying to adjust to the circus bed. One of the pieces of the serum bottle had cut you on the cheek and you were bleeding.

"He is a *macho* Mexican," said fatty.

"They just told us to get him ready and stay here until the Major arrived. Don't get all worked up," answered the pockmarked one, whose glutinous look alone kept the nurse sitting in the armchair.

The fat one scratched his chin with the sight of his pistol.

"You wouldn't have some ice and glasses around here by any chance?" the fat one asked the nurse.

The nurse looked at him fixedly.

"Fat slob, this is a hospital," she answered.

The pockmarked one came up and slapped her.

"Don't speak that way to Sergeant Robledo."

"Calm down, Malpica," said the fat one.

The door opened again and a man decked out in a plumed hat and crimson velvet cape introduced himself into the room. After him entered two others in similar dress.

The fat one could only look at them in surprise. They left no time for him to raise his pistol. The first opened his cape and there flashed a two-hand sword of Toledo steel. The subsequent thrust cleanly pierced the neck of Sergeant Robledo. The pockmarked one tried to swivel, but the nurse gave him a kick in the nuts with such good aim that he doubled over. When he tried to lift his head, three inches of steel ran through his chest.

Athos cleaned his sword on the shirt of the pockmarked one.

"Tell Aramis to come in," said the man who had entered the room first, and he gave you an enchanting smile.

"These things ought not to be happening in a hospital," said the nurse, clearly herself once more.

"We must get out of here, gentlemen. The situation may become untenable any moment," said Aramis, on entering the room. "There are more gunmen in the entrance to the hospital and one at the end of the hall."

With D'Artagnan's help you got out of bed. The nurse came up and tried to clean the cut on your cheek.

"What are you doing here?" you asked.

"The odor of this conflagration can be smelled for thousands of leagues, sir," replied Porthos.

"Miss, quickly, a stretcher," said Athos, and with a magnificent gesture swung his cape to hide his face and leave his sword free.

"Where are we going?"

"To a safe place."

The nurse winked an eye at Aramis.

THE OTHERS' VERSION
M AS IN MOVEMENT
(ONE YEAR LATER AS VIEWED
FROM YET A FURTHER YEAR)

You're driving me nuts. I accept that in accordance with your strange needs (and I accept that you must have strange needs in a place like Casablanca, Morocco; because if not, what the hell are you doing there?) I must reconstruct events, but to require me to remember the Movement of '68 as seen from the viewpoint of '69, now, in the year 1970, seems to me like madness. I swear that if it drives me crazy, it will be more from my sins than any fault of yours.

There are some people who think that to understand something allows them to put it in the drawer of nicely arranged memories and let it rest. They are the lunatics who think that a ghost can be exorcised by inviting it to dinner and requiring it to use table service and a napkin. I know several people who spent '69 in sleeplessness. I believe I was one of them, of those who allowed the anguish to accompany and change them.

I changed in '69. What do you say? No shit, it was '68 that changed me, but I changed in '69. I became less agreeable, I became more calculating in emotional things. I learned to fear the emotions.

You also withdrew inside yourself, as if by building a shell you could conserve the valor of '68, which threatened to flee from our bodies.

Typical dialogue between you and me in '69:

Me: What are you going to do this afternoon?

You: Who knows?

Me: You bought tickets for the movie?

You: I think so.

Me: Don't be a spoiled brat.

You: Yes, yes, I bought them.

Me: How many? How many did you buy?

You: Two, I bought two.

Me: Why in the hell did you buy two tickets to go to the movies if you don't have anyone to go with?

You (smiling): Because if I only gave you one, you were going to complain bitterly.

Me: Don't be a jerk. Go yourself.

You: No, you go. I don't feel like it. I want to stay and read.

Me: What theater?

You: I don't know ... At the Diana, at the Theater Diana.

Me: What's showing?

You: I wish I knew.

Me: You bought tickets at the Diana because you were walking the route our demonstrations took last year, and since there was no demonstration you were stuck, and because you didn't want your paranoid mother to ask what you were doing there you got in the line to the theater and bought two tickets.

You: And how do you know, or how did you invent that story?

Me: Because I bought tickets at the Theater Chapultepec.

You: How many?

Me: Two.

You: And who are you going with?

Me: I don't know. I think I'm going to stay and read.

You: And what are they showing at the Chapultepec?

Me: I wish I knew.

You: With what we spent on movie tickets we could have bought beer.

Me: Just so that you can see how crap-ass everything is this year.

It was a feeling. A feeling that could be described in a number of ways and a heap of memories. A feeling and a heap of memories. A feeling that you were about to take something in your hand and it escaped: water, a veil, a shadow. A feeling as if the heart were going to break and ring like a bell, and you inside the multitude. A feeling as if everything had become hyperintense.

Mother of a whore, what a cheap way to mythologize, to grow homesick. Nostalgia in bulldozer scoops.

Was it really like that? Or now does it turn out that the memory of '68 as seen from '69 is motherfucking-mystified in '70.

The truth is that we had been numerous, heroic, worthy, responsible, united, charismatic, red, giddy. At least that is what we thought of ourselves, or wanted to think, or wanted our enemies, our detractors, our parents to think. But that was in '69. In '68 we had no time to think in such inflated terms. A hundred and twenty-three days of general strike. Schools taken. Demonstrations, brigades, street assaults, meetings in Lecumberri, shots. All the walls of the city painted in a single day. Retreats, advances. The power, the revolution.

This damned letter is getting to me. I don't know what would make you think that now, in '70, I would be able to look back without being filled with the same hellish sadness.

Listen, damn you, Nestor. Why don't you come back and we'll try going out on the street again. With a sandwich board that says: *Down with bad government.* You and me alone. And the others, if we can find anyone around.

We do it and we get rid of all this shit, all this nostalgia, all this guilt for being alive and free, this guilt for having been beaten.

I leave you. I'm going to finish smoking the cigarette that I began (in order not to leave it half finished), and I'm going out in the street to see if I can find a companion who wants to come drink vermouth at my house and go to bed with me afterwards. I hope I can find one of the good ones, one of those who doesn't get scared if she wakes up in the middle of the night and finds you weeping, hugging the pillow.

See ya later, fool.

PACO IGNACIO

XIV
OF THE INSURRECTION (III)

The general headquarters had been moved to the center of the city. From the top floor of the Torre Latino-americana, in an improvised field hospital attended by a Canadian doctor who had appeared in the early morning hours and introduced himself as Norman Bethune, the revolution was carefully followed by your fingers, which held the pencil that ran over the notebooks, setting down events and issuing orders.

The appearance of the Mau Mau at the Hotel Reforma, the first thing in the morning, had allowed you to unleash a lightning attack against Lecumberri Prison, which had ended with the hanging of the director and jailors and the liberation of political and common prisoners.

A little later Doc Holliday and the Earp brothers had climbed the stairs of the Federal Security offices, firing a cloud of deadly lead and sowing their path with the bodies of agents. Coldly, the sawed-off shotgun of Doc Holliday and the Colts of the Earp brothers had opened avenues of fire in a terrifying sweep, to reappear again in the doorway, followed by a cloud of smoke and the echo of shots, unscathed, miraculously unscathed, and leaving 107 dead policemen behind them.

Menaced by a group of Tigers who served as general headquarters escort, the restaurant on the floor below had agreed to provision us with food and drink.

While the rest ate, you watched Holmes taking turns on the balconies, searching the city down there for some sign, some clue.

"The fires haven't begun, have they?"

"Not yet," replied the English detective.

"It won't be long until the mutiny breaks out. Don't worry."

"What makes you so sure?"

"I know these people. There can't be a rumble of this size without everyone wanting to get involved. We Mexicans are hot-blooded," you concluded.

"And that, what's that?" said Sherlock, pointing to the mouth of the Avenida Juárez.

You didn't have to run to one of the little telescopes mounted on the balustrade to confirm what you already knew: down Avenida Juárez came the first members of a student demonstration of 400,000.

THE OTHERS' VERSION
N *AS IN NOVELS*

Nestor, old boy:

How did you remember? It seemed like you that you would remember *Omens in the Wind*. It was my night-time obsession and many times I forced you to share it, obliging you to keep quiet while I cudgeled the Olivetti I had inherited from my uncle. But how did you remember that I had begun it seven times before giving up?

It was my novel of beginnings. Each time I started out I was full of faith, and the following day I'd read the effort and be deflated, for I didn't know what to put next. It was a bad year for writing about the year just past. All the material used in making literature should be allowed to cool. I have never been able to write while a story was still warm. It's necessary to let the bonfire go out to walk on the ashes. It may be that one of these days—if I get anything out of militancy, it will be jail or retirement—I may be able to write that novel about ourselves and '69. Could be. Meanwhile I'm sending you photocopies of the beginnings of *Omens in the Wind* and keeping the originals for myself. Just in case.

An *abrazo*,
PACO IGNACIO

P.S.: You've already told me what the sun is like. Now tell me about the moon.

P.P.S.: I've reread them. I don't think I'll ever write about the past year. The memories are growing dim. Something inside my head is working to eliminate that sad year. A Pelican eraser conspires against my nostalgia. My head emptied itself of stories and all that remains is a vague feeling that tries to synthesize empty words about the year of our defeat. I can't write about this.

OMENS IN THE WIND
By Paco Ignacio Taibo II

Chapter I

What the hell was I doing in those days?
Which days?
Those days, the ones before.
Before, it's true, before.
Well.
I was spinning around inside my head, around the shack, around the block, around the nighttime walks, around a novel, around a woman I had lost in another country, around the nights, around the Party (the construction of), around loneliness, around the faculty struggle committee, around the silence, around the mirror.
And I was going around like a madman.

OMENS IN THE WIND
By Paco Ignacio Taibo II

Chapter I

I had eaten a mess of pork tacos with my grandparents and, I don't know why, I thought that instead of taking a siesta I would sit down a while and write. It was Sunday and I had taken a seat in front of the window, trying to find a thread to start a page (it didn't matter what: a poem, an episode in a soap opera on which I was working, a subtitle for a photo, a course in Latin, whatever came). Sitting down and getting up, I had washed dirty glasses, put on and taken off records, drunk Coca-Cola and a glass of somewhat bitter wine; I had also cleaned the ashtrays and filled them with butts. But of writing, nothing, not even the last lines of my completed works would come to me.

It was Sunday and seemed more so after the meal. That was evident. Through the window I saw the closed shops and the kids playing tiddlywinks, some couples, the light of Sunday in the afternoon. But of writing, nothing. I was becoming disconsolate (which is what happens at writing tables when you can't write) when the telephone rang and I said to myself: "What luck." In two precarious jumps I reached the instrument, took down the receiver, and said:

"Mansion of the author of this novel . . ."

OMENS IN THE WIND
By Paco Ignacio Taibo II

Chapter I

Night and wind between the teeth. Light breeze, agreeable; delicious solitude accompanies the flight of your mighty bike; 58 kilos/20 years of animal traction.

Night.

Night-street empty along the whole width; the hiss, the purr of both wheels polishing the asphalt. Miguel hunching over, tuning an ear on nearing the corners to pick up the motor noise of automobiles. Nothing.

Empty streets. Miguel on the bicycle, pedaling: strong and smooth, making S's, letting himself go, little jumps on the pedal stroke. Night.

Night.

Night of stars? No, night without stars, silent.

The air hits his sweaty neck and Miguel thinks: Miguel Strogoff, the czar's mail on a bicycle, not in the DF, on the steppes of the Caucasus, ready to desert and join Putilov's division of Red Guards, under the orders of Lev Davidovich.

Arriving at the Popocatépetl traffic circle, he realizes that the fountain isn't working. Some meters further on he brakes. He approaches the bell of an old apartment building and rings. He waits. It's three in the morning. The red mail has arrived.

OMENS IN THE WIND
By Paco Ignacio Taibo II

Chapter I

We will end by inventing another city, another country, and we will walk with it stuck between our brows, a fixed vision in our eyes. Near and untrappable, distant. The old words will recover their meanings: *background, mirage, far away, there in the distance, watershed, abyss,* perhaps *wind.*

We will walk through the streets like those possessed, disconnected, alienated, sincere and decided, true crazies of the prison hospitals that the city has made immense.

And it will be inevitable. We will be the guardians, the keepers of memory in our city. We will end up carrying an M1 whose filed trigger we will constantly lick with our fingers, our conscience reposing in the sights, our outlook depending paternally on the lone ball that lies in the chamber. Ready to shoot it out with the first one who deserves it; ready for our own deaths in the name of that new city, that new country we invented (always to our sorrow, always to our shame, with a certain degree of fear of faith, of hope which, although damaging, is necessary) in a moment of carelessness that was the product of those years.

OMENS IN THE WIND
By Paco Ignacio Taibo II

Chapter I

The month was June in the city. I know what I'm telling you. I was coming back to you in loneliness, in weariness, and in an airplane.

The apparatus flew above the stain of lights, the tapestry of bonfires torn out of the darkness. The stewardess spoke your name and I snuffled as if trying to clear my head, hiding my tears, meanwhile an elderly English-woman at my side finished her last gin.

"From here, are you from here?" she asked, agreeably.

I looked at the city down below, which I still didn't love or understand very well, and to which I was returning.

OMENS IN THE WIND
By Paco Ignacio Taibo II

Chapter I

I will cross the plaza walking slowly. The wind will

dance in my ears, a lock of hair will be drawn back as if by an undertow; my eyes will measure the little paving stones, they will search out the dimensions of the square.

The plaza of the fallen one year later. Somewhere around here are the last scattered molecules of our dead brothers. In my head dance the visions of dreams, the bluish images of nightmares: the shoes lined up, the bodies lined up, the tanks lined up; the fireworks with which the slaughter began, burning in the wind, as if drawing lines in the air, as if making a scar where the scar is, where the blushing lips of the wound still await a cure.

I will walk in silence, slowly, well beyond the sound of traffic, of the guitar concert that is heard in the morning. I will walk slowly, thinking that there is the place where we meet, the point where all of us encounter each other.

OMENS IN THE WIND
By Paco Ignacio Taibo II

Chapter I

You mean that one, the ugly one, so fucked beforehand, so without opportunities? You mean that is me, that pink spot with the pointy ass and the red nose? So worthless, so fashionable, wrapped in a blue blanket and with clean diapers? You mean that? That one? Myself for always. Myself beginning shortly after the first day. That one, myself, the one in the third incubator, the one that half smiles, growls, and cries with all his soul. No, he is not ugly, he's cute as he can be. Premature? Yes, a seven-months baby. The red nose, some bruises on his body. Boy? Of course, a boy, the first. Myself crying, myself being fed by efficiently distant nurses, myself among the shadows and the lights. Myself: an inexpressive look since the 11th day of January, 1949, that observes from behind the panes of the incubator room. First discovery: am I a boy or a girl? A boy, that's great!

Myself, who does not guess that twenty years later he will walk through the plaza of the dead, searching in the air . . .

XV
THE ORGANIZED FORCES
AND THOSE WHO
HAVE TO GO ON FOOT

From a balcony of the multi-family Juárez apartments, Winnetou harangues the neighbors. Three, five thousand, eight thousand neighbors who continue growing and applaud the spirit of the insurrection. Yáñez exchanges words with the renters from the Merced, and D'Artagnan discusses matters with three thousand railway workers while standing on a Pullman at Pantaco Terminal.

It appears that the insurrection has entered its hour of truth.

The Mau Mau assault the María Isabel Sheraton and the Presidente de Hamburgo, but they're not the only ones. Over the entire city the nameless multitudes descend. They come down off the Cerro de Guadalupe, they move along the highway from Toluca, from the Molinito; they come by forced march along the turnpike from Puebla, streaming out of the "trough" of Texcoco; they leave the sand pits of Santa Fe; they desert the industrial zone of Tlalnepantla. In columns of hundreds of thousands they descend from Indios Verdes. They are the transient workers from Santa Clara, from Xalostoc, from San Juanico, from kilometer 14½, from Tulpetlac, from all Ecatepec. Those that have burns and wounds for lack of safe industrial equipment, those who were laid off in December so they wouldn't have to be paid their Christmas bonuses, those who work a sixty hour week with a pay of fifty-six, those who have been robbed of their union dues for the last fifteen years, those who were fired for wishing to form an independent union, those unjustly fined on payday by the Barapem police. They are the hordes armed with old pieces of iron, pipes and reinforcing rods; and if they're rusty, all the better. Contaminated by industrial fumes, full of the dust of the most eroded zone in Mexico City. But yes, smiling ferociously, as always. They come to the city to join the Tigers of Malaysia, who have put up barricades in the Zona de Reforma Norte and from that position resist the tank assaults of the Presidential Guard.

Those who come by the freeway assault the Port of Liverpool Department Store.

Wyatt Earp fills his saddlebags and those of his companions with crackling bills, with centennial gold pieces, and with silver coins, after sacking the National Bank of Mexico.

It is said that the general who gave the order to fire on Tlatelolco has fallen in combat. It is said that the city manager, in a desperate attempt to stop the insurrection, has ordered the poisoning of all sources of potable water in Mexico City.

But that has affected the forces of reconquest not a jot, because they have attacked the soda pop plants and are consuming the soft drinks happily, in great gulps.

The fires create a reddish, smoky afternoon. The seat of power is crumbling.

In the midst of applause the Light Brigade charges against the antiriot police. Along San Juan de Letrán the asphalt gives off sparks under the ringing hooves of the horses. The onlookers applaud, shout cheers, the lances are lowered. The police, after letting off a few timid shots (primarily to save face) scatter and flee.

People shout all over the city. Horns honk, a slow dance takes place along the avenues, confetti falls. The street vendors are making a killing.

It grows dark.

THE OTHERS' VERSION
Ñ AS IN NEWS

My dear Nestor,

Paco gave me your address and your message. I never knew that you had left Mexico. I was aware of the knife wound you got working on the newspaper, and that was all. Now Paco comes and tells me I should write to you in Casablanca, reporting on how the gang is doing.

When I went over the group of friends from '68, I realized that your situation, that of letting yourself be stabbed and then taking off for Casablanca, fell within the normal. Look at the rest.

Rolando works in a dairy in Puebla. He got married and is going to be a father. I heard that he reads like crazy (science fiction!). He's a technician and although he says he wants nothing to do with politics, I was told he's organizing an underground with the farm laborers around there. Who knows?

Of Paco you probably know as much or more than I do. He quit his public action group and wrote a novel that was rejected by four publishers. He earns his living in the strangest ways (he does magazine soap operas and radio programs that go out to doctors over closed circuit); he was married and separated six months later, betrayed and deceived, he says. He passes from euphoria to depression (more euphoria than depression, if you know him). He doesn't want to know anything about the student movement. He says that if he begins, he begins from zero and in union work (does such a thing exist?).

Marta committed suicide at the beginning of 1970. She left a note that no one could understand; she got into bed and swallowed a box of pills.

Germán disappeared. The rumor is running around that he is training in Korea.

Paco Ceja went back to being a professional student. In the mornings in Economy, and he's just entered Anthropology in the afternoons. He goes from one failed love affair to another (the optimistic cuckold saying he will learn from experience). He writes stories he shows to no one and is getting a few gray hairs.

Mario Núñez lives in France or in Switzerland. That's all I know about him. I imagine him in a big overcoat, working in a filling station or playing the harmonica on the Paris subway.

Luis Lobato went off on a scholarship to study in Italy.

María Helena left Literature and is involved in becoming a nurse. She says that she wants to do something useful. She continues the struggle which has become her life, now on a neighborhood level. It seems to be the only way for those who wish to continue the struggle, outside the traditional "isms."

The "Werewolf" got a job with Conacyt. He's still stuck on studying philosophy and walks around the department with a big pile of books under his arm. He's sure to make it. At least a doctorate. In that flight from Nezahualcóyotl that began in his adolescence, there can't be any other finish line except the Sorbonne.

I don't know who else. If I grab them all and add it up, it seems we're in a period of transition. Everyone is gone and nobody has quite finished going. All with guilt and with no way of explaining it. Something will have to happen. And with a little luck, we'll even all get together again.

An *abrazo*,
ROGELIO VIZCAÍNO

XVI
TO RETURN

While you button a shirt and tie your shoelaces for the first time in a month, you look out the window.

The city is always the same, you think. The day is gray. You wouldn't have expected it to be like that. It's a bit cold. Liliana's eyes never leave you as she smokes, sitting in the gray plastic armchair in which a few hours earlier Dick Turpin had been lodged. On putting on a black turtleneck sweater, you run your fingers over the site of the scar, proof that all this happened, proof it isn't all a dream.

At the entrance to the sanatorium a red radio-call taxi is waiting.

"And now, what are you going to do?" asks Liliana, without knowing whether to get in or say goodbye to you there and to these days together.

"I don't know."

"Are you going somewhere?"

"Yes, to Casablanca." Liliana gets in after you; the taxi pulls out.

Soon it will begin to rain. Through the window of the taxi comes the sound of horses' hooves, the muted echo of shots from Malay carbines, the clash of swords.

"Why? Why to Casablanca?"

"To return some day," you reply.

PRÉCIS OF SOME CHARACTERS

Baskervilles, Hound (of the). Dog, as its name so indicates. Main character in the novel of the same name by Sir Arthur Conan Doyle. Extraordinarily endowed to give vicious bites. His relationship with Sherlock Holmes dates from the aforementioned book.

Bethune, Norman. Communist doctor from Canada. He lent his science to the Republican side during the Spanish Civil War and later to the Chinese Revolutionary Army, died in 1942. Mao Tse Tung wrote a short account about him: "In Memory of Norman Bethune," and there exists a biography in English titled: *The Scalpel and the Sword.*

Brigade, Light (The). Is remembered in history for its absurd charge in the Battle of Balaklava, where it was decimated by Russian cannons. It has become synonymous with absurd military tactics that combine arrogance with a disregard for common sense.

D'Artagnan, Aramis, Athos, Porthos. The four musketeers who are paradoxically known as three. Alexander Dumas pére took advantage of the memories of the first to fabricate one of the most notable sagas in adventure novels. They lived in seventeenth century France and served successively Louis XIII and Louis XIV, with varying degrees of fortune. More prone to fighting than consistent in ideological matters. Ranked number one with the sword and cape.

Earp, Wyatt. Sheriff of Dodge City and Abiline in the middle of the nineteenth century. He is remembered in history for the duel in the OK Corral. Gentleman with a colt.

Earp, Virgil, Morgan, James and Bren. Brothers of the aforementioned. Their quickness on the draw and filial love form part of this legend.

Gomara, Yáñez de. Blood brother of Sandokan and creation of Emilio Salgari. Of Portuguese origin, international renegade by choice. Politically a pure anti-imperialist. Specialist in "dirty tricks." Sagacity and elegance. See the bibliographic note on Sandokan.

Holliday, Doc. Companion of the previously mentioned Earps. Many romantic legends surround him, viewing him variously as an early advocate of voluntary abortion and as a precocious member of the dispossessed. Any story of the Wild West makes a point of his black clothes, his silent presence, and his sawed-off shotgun.

Holmes, Sherlock. English detective of the nineteenth century, creation of Conan Doyle. Despite his suspicious relations with the nobility (see *Scandal in Bohemia* and *The Adventure of the Beryl Coronet*), his radical personal behavior places him nearer the revolutionary: abstainer, woman-hater, virtuoso violinist, morphine addict, specialist in the most absurd things (tobacco ashes and London mud), exceptional revolver shot. Approximate age at the time he enters our story, 45. For additional information see above all *The Sign of Four* and *A Study in Scarlet*.

The Tigers of Malaysia. A motley collection of mountain men, Malays, and blacks of the archipelago, with some island Chinese, Hispanicized Filipinos, and even a Maori and two Tibetans. They serve under the orders of Sandokan and Yáñez. Not too trustworthy in a hot game of cards (the blacks are cannibals) or poker. According to Salgari: "the fiercest forces in hand-to-hand combat."

Mau-Mau. Tribal sect of the twentieth century, originating in Kenya and profoundly involved in the anticolonial rebellion against the English, beginning in 1949. It was exterminated in a fiery bloodbath. The leaders of postcolonial reformism like Jomo Kenyatta renounced it and did away with those who had been saved from the white police.

Sandokan. Prince of Borneo. Ruler of the Island of Mompracem, general headquarters of The Tigers of Malaysia, companionable pirates who tried to put the brakes on Anglo-Dutch colonialism in the Indian Ocean and the South Pacific. Tested under fire in a thousand combats, wounded in a hundred duels. See *The Pirates of Malaysia, The Two Brothers, The King of the Sea, In the Conquest of a Kingdom, Sandokan, The Pirate's Woman* (from the series by Emilio Salgari).

Tremal Naik and Kammamuri. Companions in the adventures of the foregoing. Hunters of tigers and of men, of Hindu origin.

Turpin, Richard (Dick). English highwayman, creation of W. H. Ainsworth. The publisher Molino during the Franco era defines him as a mixture of the political delinquent and the vulgar freebooter. It appears that his phobias center on the prosperous children of the English industrial revolution. He robs nobles on the highways. Maintains excellent relations with the common people.

Tomás Rey, Moscarda, Batanero, Peters, Pat and the Knight of Malta. Companions of the foregoing. Batanero is black, Peters a redhead with sideburns, the Knight of Malta a perpetual victim of love, Tomás Rey of political persecution.

PRÉCIS OF A MOMENT

At the beginning of 1969, Gustavo Díaz Ordaz, vulture on a throne of skulls, reigned in Mexico. The student movement, massacred in the Casco de Santo Tomás, in the Plaza de la Ciudadela, in Tlatelolco, at Military Field Number One; overthrown politically because unable to ally itself with the worker movement in the great cities—was in disarray. There began the long ebb after a battle of 123 days in which thousands of Mexicans had been born as human beings.

The ebb meant a painful return of militants and leftist activists who had known moments of euphoria and liberty, to university classes; to an oppressive, defeated university in whose patios discouragement was eaten by the mouthful. It was also a return to the family, to the necessity for many of us to work and to arrange for economic survival. It was the end of student life. The crisis that affected the movement swallowed the national left and spit it out in pieces. The first popular work reforms would be delayed in taking shape for at least a couple of years. Meanwhile those who had been ceased to be.

Consciously or unconsciously, we broke with the past, refusing even to mention it. Marijuana (introduced in torrents by the government into the universities), the discouragement, the sinking of relationships by which lovers tried to lift themselves above the din of university struggles, the shifts in employment, the business opportunism, the bureaucratization of the political apparatus, the smooth turning of the mill that minced the daily lives of the middle class—did away with us as a generation. Power was further away each time; the underground dream of those who lived the Movement of '68 foundered and went out on the tide.

In defeat, we had only our isolated selves and a gray militancy as future answers to the dream of those 123 days.

Under these deplorable conditions this shortest of novels was forged. Brewed in the middle of an unseasonable divorce, the offspring of a premature marriage, of a political crisis, in an epoch of hunger and unemployment, the novel became the occasion, the vengeance, the approximation to Power by another means.

Then it was put away in a drawer and rewritten three times during the next twelve years.

PACO IGNACIO TAIBO II

Best known for his detective novels and historical writings on Mexico, Paco Ignacio Taibo II has done everything from adapting classics to comic book form, to original fiction of the highest literary order. His work has been translated into English, French, German, Italian, Polish, Bulgarian, Czechoslovak, and Russian. He and his wife and daughter make their home in Mexico City, where he is locally famous for his high consumption of cigarettes and Coca-Cola.

Taibo made his English-language debut in 1990 under a Viking imprint, with the detective novel *An Easy Thing*, which *Publishers Weekly* praised for its "complexity of social setting" and "philosophical depth."

JORGE CASTAÑEDA

A graduate of Princeton and the University of Paris, Jorge G. Castañeda is currently a professor of political science at the University of Mexico. His study *Limits to Friendship: The United States and Mexico* was published by Knopf in 1988. He is a regular columnist for the *Los Angeles Times* and *Newsweek*.

About the Translators

John Mitchell and Ruth Mitchell de Aguilar are a father and daughter team whose first collaboration, José Rubén Romero's *Notes of a Villager*, was published by Plover Press in 1988. John is the winner of a Pushcart Prize for his collection *Alaska Stories* and Ruth a full-time resident of Mexico for the last twenty years, where she runs a weaving shop in Pátzcuaro, Michoacán.